101 Social Studies Activities for Curious Kids

Written by Tracey Ann Schofield
Illustrated by Alex Glikin

Teaching & Learning Company

1204 Buchanan St., P.O. Box 10
Carthage, IL 62321-0010

This Book Belongs To

_____

Dedication

This book is for my family.
For my ancestors. For my grandparents.
For my aunts, uncles and cousins.
For my parents. For my brother.
For my husband. For my children.
For generations of special people, many of whom I never had the opportunity to meet, whose presence on the limbs and branches of my family tree have influenced my enculturation and helped to mold me into all that I am and all that I ever will be.

Special Thanks

I wish to thank my parents, Barb and Paul, for putting up with my incessant questioning about our family history; my mom for her ideas and the application of her considerable proofreading ability to my raw manuscript; my kids—Matthew, Patrick and Stephanie—for their interest in the project and their unsolicited and insightful input; my Auntie Bet for her enthusiasm and generous assistance; Patrick's grade 4 teacher, Rob Ferguson, for entrusting me with his copy of the Ontario Ministry of Education and Training's Social Studies curriculum for grades 1 to 6 (which provided the language for many of the learning concepts listed in the section overviews); Robynne Eagan for introducing me to the Teaching & Learning Company and supporting me in this solo effort; the communities of Seagrave and Port Perry for providing me with so much creative fodder; and my husband for moving a desk and computer into our living room so that I could work in a place with windows.

Cover design by Peggy Larson

Copyright © 2000, Teaching & Learning Company

ISBN No. 1-57310-262-8

Printing No. 987654321

Teaching & Learning Company
1204 Buchanan St., P.O. Box 10
Carthage, IL 62321-0010

The purchase of this book entitles teachers to make copies for use in their individual classrooms, only. This book, or any part of it, may not be reproduced in any form for any other purposes without prior written permission from the Teaching & Learning Company. It is strictly prohibited to reproduce any part of this book for an entire school or school district, or for commercial resale.

All rights reserved. Printed in the United States of America.

Table of Contents

Activity 1: Social Studies Word Search 5
Activity 2: Social Studies Crossword 6

Relationships, Rules and Responsibilities 8
Activity 3: All-Time Greats 9
Activity 4: You'd Get My Vote 10
Activity 5: Positive Power 11
Activity 6: Gone but Not Forgotten 12
Activity 7: I Wouldn't Last a Day Without You 13
Activity 8: Lifelines 14
Activity 9: Everything's Relative 15
Activity 10: A Family History 16
Activity 11: School Days 17
Activity 12: Precious Places 18
Activity 13: Extraordinary Events 19
Activity 14: Predictable Patterns 20
Activity 15: Master Plans 21
Activity 16: Oh, Baby! 22
Activity 17: Trip Tracking 23
Activity 18: Happy Holidays! 24
Activity 19: My Major Milestones 25
Activity 20: Rules Rule 26
Activity 21: House Rules 27
Activity 22: School Rules 27
Activity 23: Out and About 28
Activity 24: Playing by the Rules 29
Activity 25: A World Without Rules 29
Activity 26: Rule Makers/Rule Breakers 30
Activity 27: Cool Rules 31
Activity 28: I Have My Rights 31
Activity 29: Rights = Responsibilities 32
Activity 30: Mighty Obliged 33
Activity 31: Behaving Responsibly 34
Activity 32: It's Not My Job 35
Activity 33: Show a Little Respect 36
Activity 34: Wronged Rights 37
Activity 35: Rightful Restoration 38
Activity 36: Changing the Rules 38
Activity 37: Bask in the Glory or Suffer the
  Consequences? 39
Activity 38: Different Strokes for Different Folks 40

Traditions and Celebrations 41
Activity 39: Cultural Creatures 42
Activity 40: A Horse of a Different Color 44
Activity 41: Festive Traditions 45
Activity 42: Family Favorites 46
Activity 43: Treasured Traditions 47
Activity 44: Breaking with Tradition 48
Activity 45: Family Name Game 48
Activity 46: Story Savers 49
Activity 47: Intergalactic Tradition Transmission 49
Activity 48: Hunting for Heritage 50
Activity 49: Family "Hair"looms 50
Activity 50: You've Got Your Mother's Eyes 51
Activity 51: The Luck of the Irish 51
Activity 52: Heritage Days 52

Activity 53: Flying High 53
Activity 54: Aesthetics/Athletics 54
Activity 55: Food for Thought 54
Activity 56: Cultural Comparisons 55
Activity 57: Delicious Diversity 56
Activity 58: Cultural Celebrations Community Style 56
Activity 59: Community Contributions 57

Days Gone By 58
Activity 60: More Fun, Less Work? 59
Activity 61: Easier or Harder? 59
Activity 62: From Post and Beam to Bricks and Mortar ... 60
Activity 63: Cool Tools 60
Activity 64: Here's to Your Health 61
Activity 65: Talk and Travel 61
Activity 66: Fun and Frolic 62
Activity 67: The Evolution of Food 62
Activity 68: Signs of the Times 63
Activity 69: Create a Coat/Bill/Coin/Stamp 63
Activity 70: Back in Time 64

My Community 65
Activity 71: Needy Beings 66
Activity 72: Super Structures 66
Activity 73: People at Work 67
Activity 74: Safe and Sound 68
Activity 75: Getting Around 68
Activity 76: Secret Systems 69
Activity 77: Special Places 69
Activity 78: Community Central 70
Activity 79: Volunteers Are VIPs 70
Activity 80: My Community, My School and Me 71
Activity 81: Finding My Way 71
Activity 82: Follow Me 72
Activity 83: Junior Cartographers (Mini Mapmakers) 74
Activity 84: A-1 Coordination 75
Activity 85: No Place Like Home 76

The Global Village 78
Activity 86: A Small Part of the Big Picture 79
Activity 87: Popular Percentages 83
Activity 88: Never Eat Shredded Wheat (N, S, E, W) 85
Activity 89: The City Kid and the Country Kid 86
Activity 90: Location, Location, Location! 87
Activity 91: Back and Forth 88
Activity 92: En-Dependent 88
Activity 93: Climate Controlled 89
Activity 94: Planet Protectors 90
Activity 95: Who Does What Where? 91
Activity 96: Trade-Offs 92
Activity 97: One Big, Happy Family 93
Activity 98: Prodigious Producers 93
Activity 99: Seeing the World 94
Activity 100: Conscientious Contributions 95
Activity 101: Time in a Bottle 95
Answer Key 96

Dear Teacher or Parent,

As educators and parents, social studies challenges us to provide our children with an exciting, relevant and thorough examination of communities that will give them the information and understanding they require to become responsible adult citizens in a culturally diverse and interdependent world. To this end, it is critical that we offer a school program and home environment that encourages the development of a positive attitude toward learning; respect, tolerance and understanding of individuals, groups and cultures in the global community; respect and responsibility for the environment; and an understanding and appreciation of the rights, privileges and responsibilities of citizenship.

With *101 Social Studies Activities for Curious Kids*, children first develop an understanding of the familiar worlds of home and school through past, present and future self-directed written and oral explorations. Moving on in later chapters to the dynamic and complex world that exists outside the classroom and the home, children relate what they have learned about their own identity and values to the larger regional, national and international context. Children should be given a chance to read their responses out loud. By encouraging children to share their work with their peers, we give them an opportunity to evaluate different points of view and to examine issues critically with an eye to solving problems and making decisions on important issues that affect their lives.

When kids recognize the value and relevance of what they are learning, they are motivated to work and learn effectively. Like the other books in the *101 Activities* series, *101 Social Studies Activities for Curious Kids* allows children to explore a subject by writing about what they know and understand best —themselves. Using personal experience as a springboard for creative thinking, children need little or no adult direction to examine "Relationships, Rules and Responsibilities," "Traditions and Celebrations," "Days Gone By," "My Community" and "The Global Village" in a meaningful, rich and relevant context. To kickstart dormant creative juices, a written example, which can be read aloud, accompanies each activity (except where the desired response is objective rather than subjective or where an example might limit children to my critical thinking pathway) and a word search and crossword puzzle at the beginning of the book use the same key words and concepts to introduce kids to the language of social studies.

With direct curriculum links to English, history, geography and mathematics, *101 Social Studies Activities for Curious Kids* provides teachers and parents with an excellent opportunity to reinforce learning while giving children something fun to do. Responses to each activity can be short or lengthy and can take minutes or hours, depending on the writer's individual level of ability, interest and enthusiasm. Contrary to the prevailing attitude of today's youth, social studies can be fun. I hope you and your children find *101 Social Studies Activities for Curious Kids* to be a useful and enjoyable tool, and take as much delight in travelling the pathway to social enlightenment and civic mindedness as much as I did!

Sincerely,

Tracey

Tracey Ann Schofield

Activity 1

Social Studies Word Search

Find the words listed and circle them in the puzzle. The words can be forward, backward, up, down or diagonally.

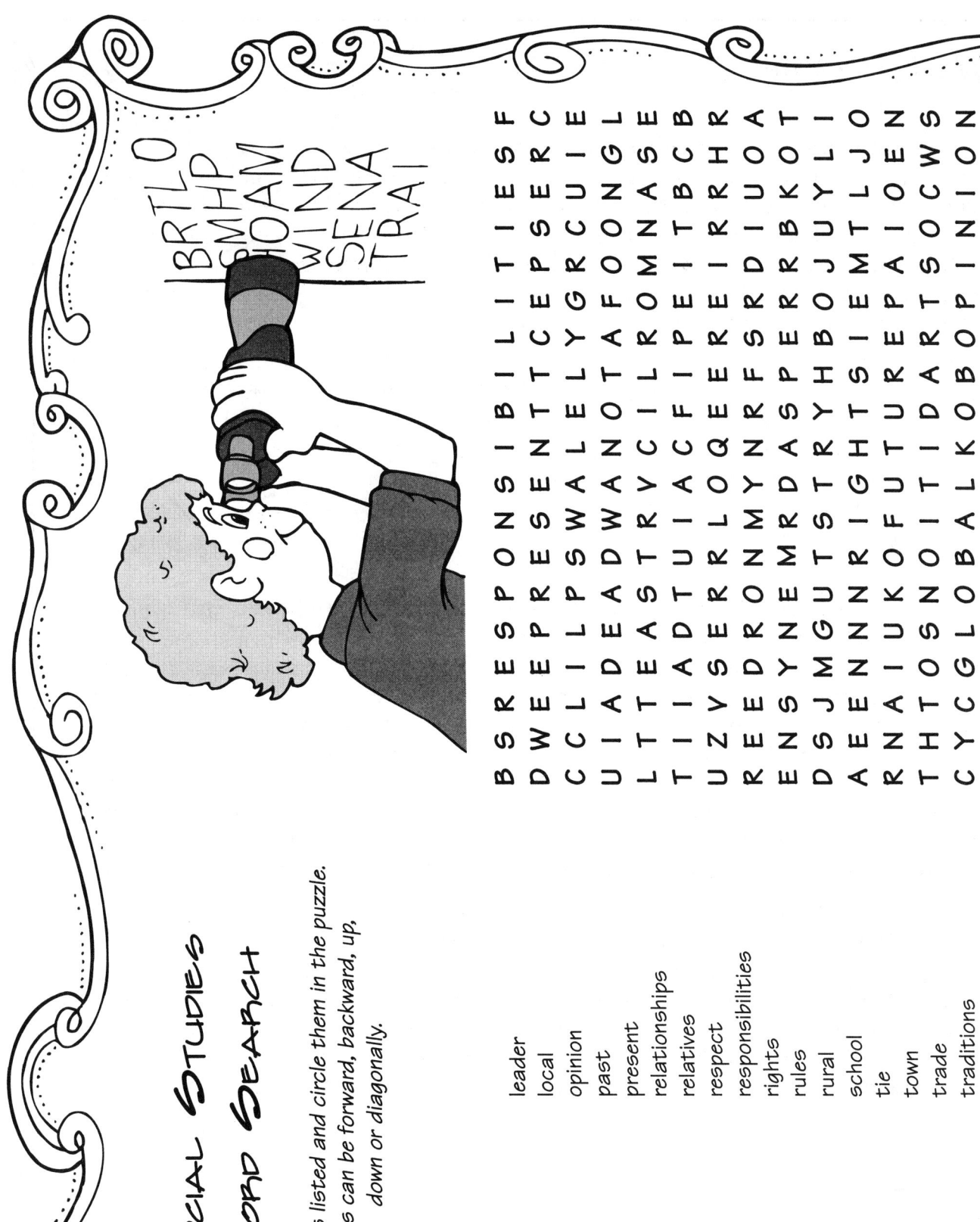

```
B S R E S P O N S I B I L I T I E S F
D W E E P R E S E N T T C E P S E R C
C C L L P S W A L E L Y G R C U I E U
U I A D E A D W A N O T A F O O N G L
L T T E A S T R V C I L R O M N A S E
T I A D T U I A C F I P E I T B C B R
U Z V S E R R L O Q E E R E I R R H R
R E E D R O N M Y N R F S R D I U O A
E N S Y N E M R D A S P E R R B K O T
D S J M G U T S T R Y H B O J U Y L I
A E E N N N R I G H T S I E M T L J O
R N A I U K O F U T U R E P A I O E N
T H T O S N O I T I D A R T S O C W S
C Y C G L O B A L K O B O P I N I O N
```

celebrations
change
citizens
city
community
contribution
cooperation
country
culture
duty
environment
flag
friends
future
global
heritage
ideas
job
laws
leader
local
opinion
past
present
relationships
relatives
respect
responsibilities
rights
rules
rural
school
tie
town
trade
traditions
urban

Activity 2

Social Studies Crossword

Across

2. not today sometime down the road
4. an urban center
6. a group of people who enjoy the same privileges and live in the same locality under the same laws
9. having formerly been; gone by
10. a binding rule established by authority
11. to alter; to cause to be different
12. esteem; to have deferential regard for; to honor and ___
17. special privileges enjoyed in accordance with truth, justice and law and balanced with responsibilities
18. an educational institution
19. country life; not urban
20. a piece of light cloth bearing a symbolic design and used to indicate nationality
23. connection by birth or marriage; kinship
24. one's native land or the land of one's citizenship
25. not distant, close by; restricted to or characteristic of a particular place
26. an element of a culture passed down through generations
28. a belief or conclusion confidently held but not substantiated by knowledge or proof
30. work; occupation
31. things done in commemoration of any event
33. a person you like, trust and respect and who likes, trusts and respects you
34. today; not in the past

Down

1. people who are in charge or exercise control and influence
3. things for which you are accountable; duties, trusts or debts
4. learned behavior of people, including belief systems and languages
5. any collection of houses and buildings bigger than a village but not incorporated as a city
7. a connection
8. inherited qualities or characteristics; any condition or culture which is allotted or handed down
11. something that is given in common with others or given for a common purpose
13. the conditions affecting the existence, growth and welfare of living things; one's surroundings
14. established method; a standard, principle, regulation, guide or formula for procedure or conduct
15. joint action; working together for mutual benefit
16. involving the entire world
21. pertaining to or characteristic of a city; opposite of rural
22. a kinsman; a member of your family
27. mercantile traffic; commerce; the profitable exchange of goods and services
29. notions or thoughts
32. ethical, moral or legal obligation

Relationships, Rules and Responsibilities

In this section, students identify significant people, places and events in their lives and describe simple patterns that influence their daily existence. They also examine rules, rights and responsibilities in their home, school and neighborhood. Specifically, they . . .

- identify important people in their country, both past and present (Activities 3-5)
- identify important past and present relationships in their lives (Activities 6, 7)
- construct a time line identifying the history of a family member or a special person (Activity 8)
- construct a simple family tree identifying family members (Activity 9)
- create a simple time line to show relevant family/school history (Activities 10-11)
- describe significant places in their lives (Activity 12)
- identify significant events in their lives (Activity 13)
- describe simple patterns that influence their daily lives (Activities 14-16)
- order a sequence of events orally and with pictorial symbols (Activities 17-19)
- identify rules in the home, at school and in the community (Activities 20-23)
- demonstrate an understanding of the need for rules and responsibilities (Activities 24-27)
- identify and describe the rights and responsibilities of family members, group members and members of the community (Activities 28-31)
- demonstrate an understanding of rights and responsibilities in a way that shows respect for the rights and property of other people (Activities 32-35)
- explain how rules and responsibilities may change over time (Activity 36)
- recognize and describe the consequences of events and actions that affect their lives (Activity 37)
- identify the factors that might cause rules to change and describe the changes (Activity 38)

Activity 3

All-Time Greats

1. List the 10 most important people ever to play a leading role in your country and note at least one major accomplishment for each. These people can be explorers, inventors, politicians, doctors, soldiers, civil rights activists, environmentalists . . . anyone who has helped to bring about a change that has made your country a better place to live. (If you are stuck, look in an encyclopedia or ask someone else in your house for his or her opinions and rationale.)

2. List 10 celebrities who have brought recognition to your country and describe at least one of their notorious (widely known) achievements. These can be artists, actors, writers, athletes, musicians, comedians, dancers. (Your celebrity list can be restricted to one category or cover a number of categories.)

Example: 10 of Canada's Most Important Leaders
1. Sir John A. MacDonald: Canada's first Prime Minister and one of the Fathers of Confederation.
2. Alexander Graham Bell: inventor of the telephone and phonograph and founder of the National Geographic Society.
3. Frederick Banting (and Charles Best): researcher (and assistant) who discovered how to manufacture insulin for the treatment of diabetes.
4. Terry Fox: cancer victim who heightened awareness of the disease through his cross-Canada "Marathon of Hope" and who is posthumously responsible for millions of treatment and cure fund-raising dollars.
5. Dr. Daniel David Palmer: teacher and healer who performed the first chiropractic adjustment and is considered to be the founder of chiropractic medicine.
6. J.-Armand Bombardier: inventor and manufacturer of "tracked vehicles for transport over snow-covered terrains," or the snowmobile.
7. George Brown: founder and first publisher of *The Globe and Mail*, Canada's national newspaper.
8. Lester B. Pearson: Prime Minister and Nobel Peace prize winner.
9. Lord Simcoe: founder of the city of Toronto (his wife, Lady Simcoe, was Toronto's greatest early historian).
10. Brian Mulroney: Prime Minister who negotiated the North American Free Trade Agreement (NAFTA).

Activity 4

You'd Get My Vote

Interview someone who is at least 25 years your senior. Ask him or her to tell you about the most important person to lead the country when he or she was younger (the person who had the greatest impact). What were some of this leader's most memorable moments? What were some of his or her best and worst decisions? If you could, would you support this leader today? Why or why not?

Example: John Fitzgerald Kennedy: President of the United States of America

Best/Worst Decisions

- established the Peace Corps to help people in developing countries
- initiated disastrous Bay of Pigs invasion by Cuban rebels against their homeland
- championed civil rights and proposed many legislative changes to end segregation and racial discrimination
- promoted the development of space exploration

Memorable Moments

- coining of the phrase "ask not what your country can do for you, ask what you can do for your county" in his 1961 inaugural address.
- picture published around the world as he addressed German citizens at City Hall in West Berlin with the words Ich bin ein Berliner.
- appointed a Special Advisor to the Arts and invited many celebrated artists to perform at the White House.

My Feelings

Would I vote for him today? Probably. it is easy, now, to see the mistakes that were made and to find fault with policies and decisions. But John F. Kennedy, then or now, was an imposing political figure–intelligent, charming, handsome, from a powerful and polished family. People voted for him not only for what he said but how he said it–and probably would again.

As with many politicians, JFK's supporters felt that he changed the U.S. for the better while his detractors felt that he changed it for the worse. But all mourned the loss of the young, charismatic president when he was assassinated on November 21, 1963, in Dallas, Texas.

Activity 5

Positive Power

Who is the political leader of your community, state (or province) or country today? What has he or she done to make your home a better place? Is he or she a good leader?

Example 1: Mike Harris: Premier of Ontario

- has restructured government spending to reduce the provincial deficit and regain Ontario's preferential loan status
- has improved the efficiency and quality of Ontario's educational and health care systems
- has restructured and regionalized the province's bureaucracy

I think Mike Harris has done a difficult job well, greatly improving Ontario's economic climate and recharting the province's social course. Many of his decisions are unpopular, and he has been accused of going too far too fast, but I think you have to give credit to a man who was handed a bushel basket of rotten apples and had the foresight and courage to make applesauce.

Example 2: Ima Towne Cownslar*

Mrs. Cownslar has done many great things for our community during her two years in public office. In particular, she has improved the "youth-friendliness" of our town, focusing on the promotion of healthy and productive diversions for local kids. Ima has taken a tough stand on youth crime, directing funds to after-school and evening programming for pre-teens and teenagers. She has lobbied for tougher anti-smoking by-laws and increased spending on programs designed to keep kids in school and off the street. She has approved plans for a new community, center, is an active member of the Skateboard Park Fund-Raising Committee and sits on the board of directors for the local recreational mixed teen softball league. She has also implemented a youth job training program that sponsors weekend workshops on small business start-up for teens. A vote for Mrs. Cownslar is a vote for our future. If Ima runs for re-election, she will definitely get my vote.

*Ima Towne Cownslar is a fictional character.

Activity 6

Gone but Not Forgotten

Describe the important relationship you had with someone (or something) who (that) is no longer in your life: a grandparent who died; a friend who moved away; a teacher at an old school; a pet you had to give away; an old toy you broke, lost or sold at a garage sale... What made your relationship special? Why will you never forget the times you spent together? What important lessons did you learn from your relationship? What effect does this relationship have on your life today?

(Try to write your answer in paragraph form.)

Example: Still

My best friend Judy died tragically in her early thirties. She is gone, but I will never forget the 25 years we shared together. Although we lived apart for much of that time, we always kept in touch, by letter, by telephone, by cassette tape, by bus. We had so many adventures. Rarely, if ever, did we quarrel. She knew everything about me, and I knew everything about her. I even saved her life once. Judy taught me so much about kindness and what it means to be a good friend. I was terrible at keeping in touch, too busy, too wrapped up in my own small world, but she always maintained contact. She never gave up on me, never stopped calling, never cast me aside, never punished me for making her do all the work. She taught me to answer the phone, even when I didn't feel like talking; to make the trip, even when I didn't feel like driving; to make the effort even when I felt too tired. She showed me that it was possible to love another person unconditionally, to give everything and expect little or nothing in return. She has been dead for many years, but I still feel her presence in my life. Sometimes she visits me in my dreams. At Christmastime, she still makes the long trip to our house to share a little holiday cheer with my family. On loan from Heaven for the day, I feel her there, beside me, unwrapping presents, joining in the festivities. Her gifts surround me. Small things: a framed picture of the two of us, smiling, on my wedding day; a good luck rock; a baby's bedside light. And memories: of a tricycle and a brick wall, an apartment railing and a line-up of tiny toads, a rock concert and a pair of opera glasses, a dude ranch and a three-day horseback ride. These things I will never forget. Her laughter still rings in my ears. Her generosity still warms my heart. Her friendship still fills my soul. I can see her round, kind face before me, young and smiling. I can feel the softness of her cheek as I kiss her hello or good-bye. In a way it is just like old times. Apart, but together. Still.

Activity 7

I Wouldn't Last a Day Without You

List the reasons why you wouldn't last a day without that special someone (or something) in your life: your mom or dad, your brother or sister, your best friend, your teacher, your coach, your pet, your teddy bear.
(You can use bullets or paragraph form.)

Examples: I wouldn't last a day without my kids
I wouldn't last a day without my kids. Although it would be blissfully quiet, I would miss their constant chatter. I would miss their hugs and kisses, the closeness of their bodies, their words of encouragement. I would miss cuddling them at night. I would miss their questions—and their answers. I would miss their smell. I would miss their laughter. I would miss their tears and the way only I can dry them. I would miss their baseball games. I would miss grocery shopping and holding their small hands. What would I do if they were no longer in my life? My days would be empty without their debris: the mountains of laundry, the dirty dishes, the uneaten meals. My heart would crumble. My whole being would ache for the wanting of them. I would crave their mess and their complications. And, although it seems impossible, I might even come to miss their bickering, their jostling for position, their wrestling and their verbal sparring. Without them to keep my mind vital and alive, I would atrophy. I would forget to feel energetic and dependable and vibrant and capable and loving. I would forget how to gaze at life longingly with expectancy and innocence. I would forget how to look forward to tomorrow through the exhaustion of today. I would forget how to be a mother.

I wouldn't last a day without my husband, Jonathan, **because:**

- who else would put up with my constant griping, insecurities and artistic longings?
- who else would say, "You look great" when I weigh in at 200 pounds?
- who else would struggle to keep me in the style to which I would like to become accustomed?
- who else would understand that I still don't know what I want to be when I grow up?
- who else would wash my car or unplug the toilet or kill a spider on the ceiling?
- who else would bring me back t-shirts from 10 different countries every year?
- who else would "listen" to me and read a magazine and watch TV at the same time?
- who else would let me continue to spend money even when we don't have any?
- who else would roughhouse with the kids because I would rather read to them?
- who else would tell me that I have great parents—and mean it?
- who else would say, "That was delicious" when I'd burnt dinner black?
- who else would crawl around on the floor for hours pretending to be a lion?
- who else would build science projects out of scraps of wood and bits of string?
- who else would watch the same car race over and over and still find it exciting?
- who else would ruffle my hair and call me a "big goof"?
- who else would tell me that I am a great mom?
- who else would be my best friend and lifelong companion?
- who else would be my husband?

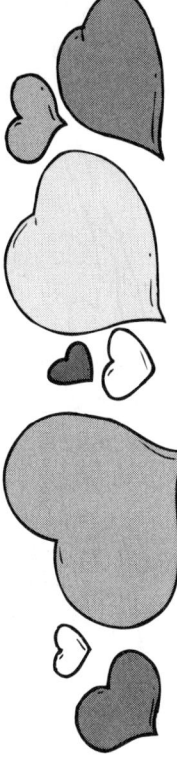

Activity 8

LIFELINES

Create a time line that highlights and commemorates the history of a family member or a special person. Draw a picture of this individual. (It is easier if you make a list of the events first, before you put them on a time line. It helps you to organize and sequence the events and determine the number of event lines you will have to draw, and it saves a lot of erasing on the line itself. It also gives you the opportunity to eliminate some of the lesser important entries if you find yourself with too many. Don't forget, you can put your writing above and below the line. If you alternate—one up, one down—it allows you to fit more words on your time line.)

Example: The History of Barbara Ann Gordon (My Mom)

- **1938:** Barbara Ann "Gordie-bear" is born
- **1940:** has tonsils out on kitchen table (mother assists and goldfish dies from the ether)
- **1951:** wins penmanship contest at Gledhill P.S.
- **1954:** meets future husband and gets first summer job
- **1955:** wins shorthand medal at Malvern Collegiate Institute, graduates from grade 12 and gets first full-time job
- **1958:** marries Paul Coveart
- **1960:** buys first house for $15,000 at 90 Fenelon Drive
- **1963:** gives birth to daughter, Tracey Ann
- **1965:** gives birth to son, Matthew Gordon
- **1965:** witnesses father retire after 40 years with the Metropolitan Toronto Police Force
- **1967:** travels by bus to Expo '67 in Montreal
- **1969:** develops arthritis
- **1974:** loses father to cancer
- **1976:** receives a tennis serve in the glasses and gets glass fragments in the eye
- **1985:** marries daughter, Tracey, to Jonathan Schofield
- **1987:** welcomes first grandchild (Matthew Schofield) and says good-bye to mother (Vera Gordon), mother-in-law (Geraldine Coveart), dog of 16 years (Bun) and uncle-in-law (John Coveart)
- **1990:** welcomes second grandchild (Patrick Schofield)
- **1991:** welcomes third grandchild (Stephanie Schofield) and marries son, Matthew to Linda McGarry
- **1995:** welcomes fourth grandchild (Taylor Coveart) and witnesses husband's retirement
- **1996:** retires from Southam Communications
- **1997:** sells first house for $186,000 and buys log home on 8.5 rural waterfront acres
- **1998:** welcome fifth grandchild (Ryan Coveart)

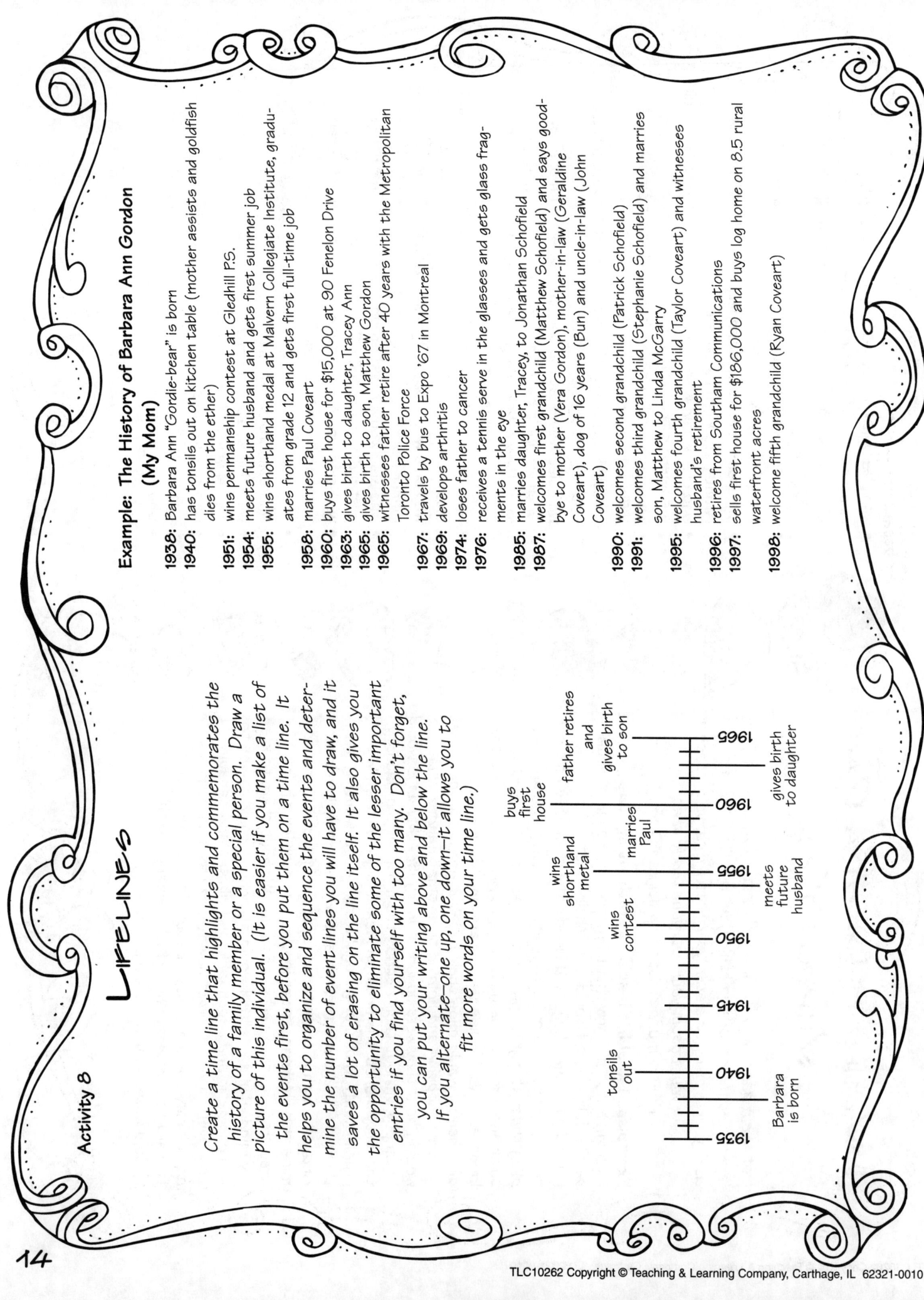

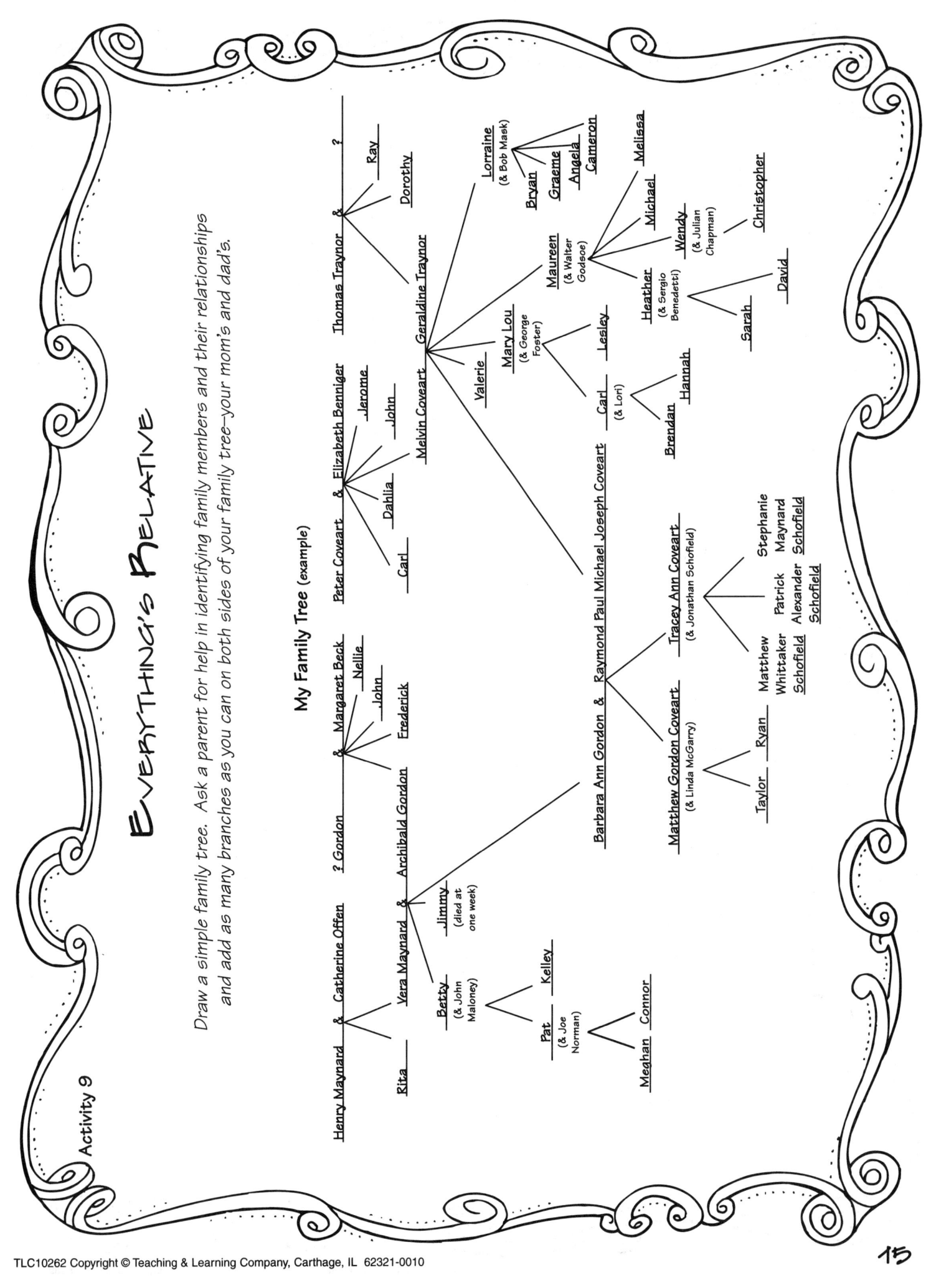

Activity 10

A Family History

Using words and dates, create a time line of your family history. Start with the date of your birth and include such important events as births, deaths, marriages, divorces, new homes, new schools, new jobs, new pets, new siblings, special vacations, athletic/academic/artistic achievements, religious milestones. (Make sure you make a list of events before plotting them on your time line.)

Example: Tracey's Family History Time Line

1963: I am born.
1965: My brother, Matthew, is born.
1968: I start public school.
1971: We lose our family cottage and buy a camper; The Toronto Telegram closes and my Dad is out of work.
1972: Dad starts his own printing company, T & M Typesetting, and we get our dog, Bun.
1974: Grandpa Gordon dies and Dad starts work as a machinist at The Globe and Mail.
1975: We take our first camping trip to Disney World and my Auntie Lou dies.
1976: We take our first camping trip out west, and I start junior high.
1977: We take our first camping trip out east.
1978: My Aunt Valerie dies and I start high school.
1979: My Uncle John dies.
1982: I graduate from high school and start college.
1983: I transfer to the University of Toronto.
1984: I get my first apartment.
1985: I graduate from the university, marry Jonathan and move to Ottawa.
1986: My Grandma Gordon moves into a nursing home.
1987: I move to Arnprior, give birth to Matthew and lose my grandmothers.
1988: We take our first trip to the Schofield cottage in Nova Scotia.
1990: I give birth to Patrick and we build our dream home in Braeside.
1991: I give birth to Stephanie and my brother gets married.
1992: Stephanie is diagnosed with "global development delay" and a seizure disorder.
1993: I turn 30 and take a three-day horseback ride with my best friend.
1995: My dad retires from The Globe and Mail; my nephew, Taylor, is born; I celebrate my 10th wedding anniversary and my best friend, Judy, dies.
1996: My mom retires from Southam Communications and we move to Whitby.
1997: My mom and dad leave their home of 37 years and move to Seagrave.
1998: My nephew, Ryan, is born and my mom and dad celebrate their 40th anniversary.
1999: We move to Seagrave.
2000: My family, along with the rest of the world, ushers in the new millennium.

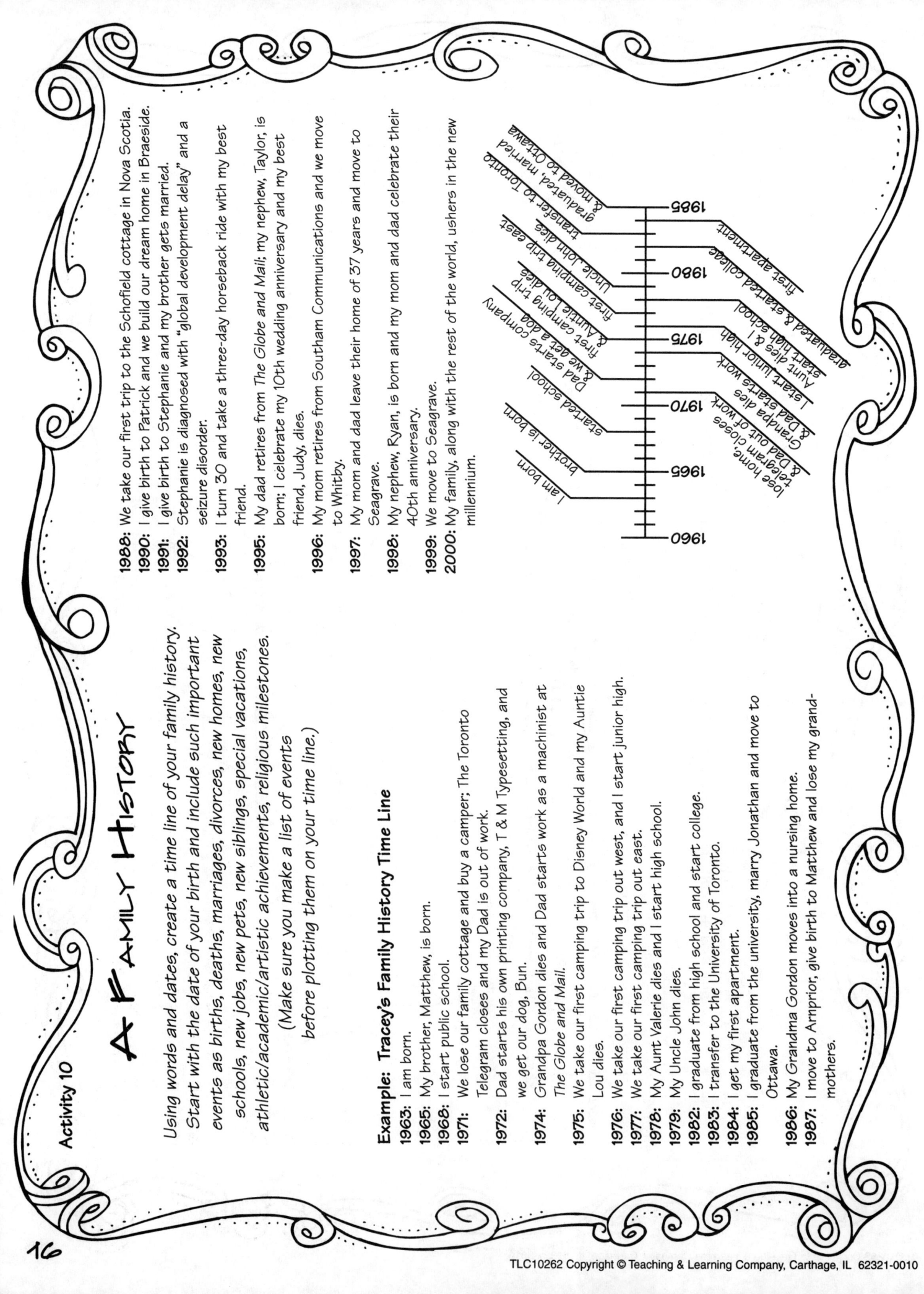

Activity 11

School Days

Find out what year your school opened. Write a time line to record your school's history. Include dates (years or years and months) for such events as: the welcoming of key new staff members—principals/vice principals, teachers, librarians, custodians; the establishment of playgrounds and gardens; the introduction of extracurricular programs; major athletic/artistic/academic achievements; major excursions; special awards and ceremonies; the installation of the first computer; the establishment of home and school groups; the construction of the first portable or any additions; enrollment highlights . . .

(Before creating your time line, make a list of important events.)

Example: Rene Gordon (formerly Karen Road) Public /School*

1964: Karen Road Public School opens its doors.
1966: Trees are planted in front of school.
1968: School population reaches 400.
1969: Library is expanded.
1970: Soccer pitch established in school field.
1971: School hosts fun fair to raise money for the purchase of "Karen the Kangaroo" for the Metro Toronto Zoo.
1972: Mr. Talon starts school choir.
1973: Rumor has it that one of the zoo's penguins, purchased with subsequent fun fair money, escapes its enclosure and is eaten by a lion. In truth, a number of penguins die from ingesting pennies thrown into their swimming pool.
1975: First principal, Mr. Carruthers, retires and is replaced by Mr. Johnston.
1976: Tetherball pole is installed.
1985: Day care opens in school.
1989: School name changed to Rene Gordon Public School in memory of beloved school trustee and parent.
1999: Twenty-five-year reunion.

*These dates are approximations and some events are fictitious.

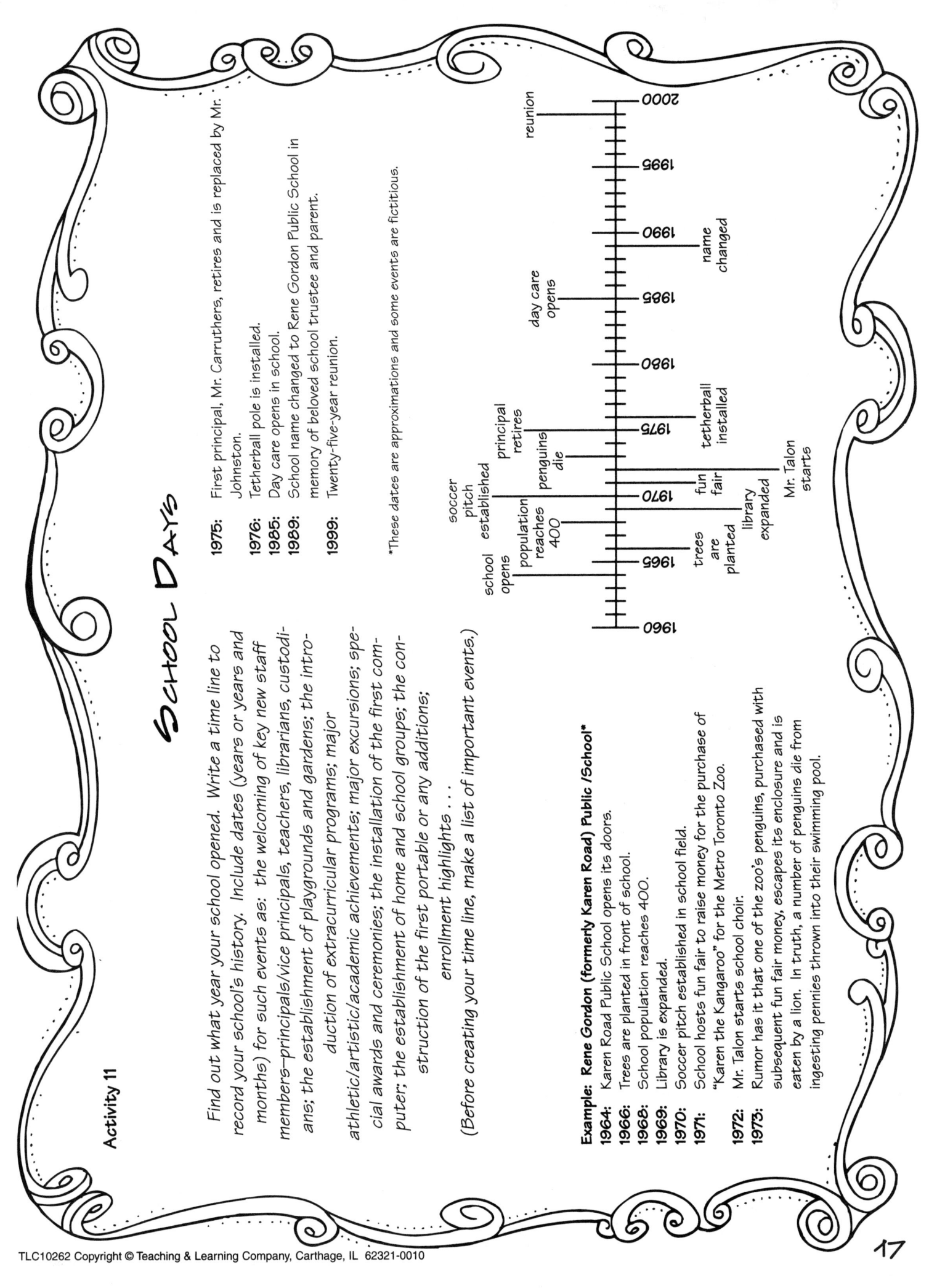

Activity 12

Precious Places

Describe one of the most important places in your life: your bedroom, your kitchen, your classroom, your backyard, your grandma's apartment, the park, the hockey arena, the beach . . .

Example: My Garden

My garden is one of the most important places in my life. Watching my plants come back year after year fills me with a sense of hope and gives me something to look forward to over the long winter months. I love to watch the green shoots push themselves out of the rich dark earth on the first sunny spring days. I love to watch the slender green stems unfurl and the leaf buds bulge and explode. I love to watch the flower buds developing, swelling and then splitting to reveal blossoms of extraordinary color and fragrance and beauty. I love to watch the bumblebees land on those flower heads and fill their pollen sacs as they probe the bloom for nectar. I love digging the earth and making a little hollow for a new plant. I love to pack the dirt around the delicate stalk and watch my new addition take root and thrive. I love to turn a wild patch of weeds and grass with a shovel, to knock the dirt and worms from the tangled roots, to create a fresh bed of fertile soil and to fill it with hungry, thirsty, determined life. Whenever I move my family to a new home, I always take some of our established perennial plants with us. The first thing I do–before I even unpack–is to prepare the new garden and transplant my memories. It gives me a sense of continuity. When I see new spring life in the little spot where I planted my old chives, violets, daisies, poppies, columbine, peonies and clematis, I remember all of the lovely places I have lived and gardened. My childhood home, where the violets took over the shady front bed; my Whitby home where I mowed around daisies that had seeded in the grass. And I remember the people with whom I have shared my life. My grandfather, who grew the ancestors of the poppies that thrive in my garden today; my grandmother, who started those assertive purple violets so many years before; my father, who brought back a packet of columbine seeds from British Columbia more than 20 years ago; my mother, who split her beautiful pink peony bush so that I could take something of her with me when I moved away from home; my children, who presented me with a tiny, climbing clematis in a garden center pot one Mother's Day. My garden is a place of hope, of joy, of beauty and of happy reminiscence. My garden is a precious place.

Activity 13

Extraordinary Events

Write about a memorable event or something really important that happened to you: your first day of school, your first goal, a great report card, meeting your best friend, getting a new pet, the day your baby brother was born, your bout with chicken pox, a really good deed . . . .

Example: My Wedding Day

My wedding day was one of the happiest of my life and one that I will never forget. August 3, 1985, was excruciatingly humid. We were delivered by horse-drawn carriage to the minute 150-year-old white frame church at Black Creek Pioneer Village. My aunts let the horses in the field wear their fancy hats and took a picture. A number of the guests went to the wrong church and bolted from their seats when they did not recognize the bride who was walking down that aisle. We held off until they arrived, and apologized to the other wedding party later. To ease my nervousness, the church caretaker told my father and me a story that took so long our guests (and the groom) almost ran down the small aisle to make up for lost time and could see my mom mouthing the words "slow down!" My groom and I sweated through our vows to the sound of my maid of honor's inconsolable weeping. My great uncle, one of Canada's foremost concert pianists, provided the musical accompaniment. After the ceremony, the caretaker opened up the old gristmill so we could have our picture taken above the paddle wheel on a little wooden balcony. My husband and I then posed with the horses in harness. He was terrified. I laughed out loud and the photographer snapped one of my favorite wedding pictures. We bounced our way to The Halfway House, the pioneer inn where our reception was held. The meal was wonderful. My husband made a very funny ad-lib speech. People had to sing to get us to kiss. We danced to "How Do You Make the Music Last?" from the movie *Best Friends* and the DJ played "Big Joe Mufferaw" (who paddled up the Madawa all the way from Ottawa in just one day) by Stompin' Tom Connors for our Ottawa guests. My brother and his friends sang "Ging Gang Goo," the little green frog song that is their wedding tradition. I danced like crazy to "I Knew the Bride When She Used to Rock and Roll." We stayed very late enjoying the company of our friends and family. By the time we left, the park was closed. We were trapped! My grandma found an exit, but had to navigate a six-foot drop. We were luckier. We found the park gates. It wasn't until my husband had scaled 20 feet of wrought iron and dropped to the ground on the other side that we realized the gate was unlocked! Exhausted, but happy, we finally made it back to our car. When my husband turned the key in the ignition, thousands of pieces of confetti came spilling out of the ventilation system. For years afterward, little paper circles would occasionally fly up in our faces, and we would think of my brother-in-law's practical joke and our wonderful, wonderful wedding day.

Activity 14

Predictable Patterns

Describe a simple pattern that you follow over the course of a day, week or month.

pattern: a model from which to copy or imitate

Example: My School Day/Work Day Pattern

- **7:00 a.m.:** let Stephanie drag me out of bed, get dressed and put in my contact lenses
- **7:05 a.m.:** get Stephanie her breakfast
- **7:06 a.m.:** try to wake up Matthew and Patrick for the first time
- **7:10 a.m.:** dress Stephanie
- **7:15 a.m.:** brush Stephanie's hair
- **7:20 a.m.:** make Stephanie's lunch
- **7:25 a.m.:** pack Stephanie's school bag
- **7:30 a.m.:** try to wake up Matthew and Patrick again
- **7:35 a.m.:** kiss Stephanie good-bye and put her on the bus
- **7:40 a.m.:** physically drag the boys out of bed
- **7:41 a.m.:** (and every minute thereafter) yell, "Hurry up; we're going to be late!"
- **7:42 a.m.:** find Patrick some clean clothes in the pile on his bedroom floor
- **7:45 a.m.:** make the boys' lunches
- **7:50 a.m.:** make sure the boys are eating their breakfast and not fighting
- **7:55 a.m.:** find both boys some socks
- **7:56 a.m.:** sign Patrick's agenda so he doesn't have to write out his spelling words five times
- **8:00 a.m.:** rush the boys to their bus stop with moments to spare
- **8:05 a.m.:** kiss the boys good-bye and watch them cross the highway to the bus
- **8:06 a.m.:** wave to the boys in their seats on the bus
- **8:09 a.m.:** watch the bus drive out of sight
- **8:10 a.m.:** go back home and change into my jogging shoes
- **8:15 a.m.:** walk/jog 2.5 miles (stopping to visit with my parents at the halfway point)
- **9:00 a.m.:** cool down by wandering around and praising my trees and plants on their growth
- **9:05 a.m.:** stroke, feed and water outdoor cats, Sam and Monty
- **9:10 a.m.:** feed two bowls of fighting fish, a tank of guppies and a turtle
- **9:15 a.m.:** wolf down a bowl of cereal with 1% milk
- **9:20 a.m.:** grab a quick shower
- **9:30 a.m.:** get dressed again
- **9:35 a.m.:** start working at my computer
- **9:36 a.m.:** answer the phone for the first time (it will then ring once every 10 minutes)
- **1:30 p.m.:** eat a calorie-wise freezer lunch and read *National Geographic* magazine
- **2:00 p.m.:** return to my computer
- **3:30 p.m.:** carry Stephanie off the bus
- **3:31 p.m.:** start my real job!

Master Plans

Write about the 24-hour day/night cycle, the seven-day week or the changing of the seasons. What is the pattern that repeats itself over and over again? How does this pattern exercise control over your life?

Example: The 12-Month Year

Every 30 or 31 days (28 or 29 in February) we turn a page of our 12-month calendar. Once each month, we have to pay our utility bills, our taxes and our mortgage. I get paid once a month and receive funding for Stephanie's special services at-home worker. Each month generally offers at least one special event or holiday that we anticipate and celebrate. We count down to see how many more months it is until our next birthday—even when our last birthday was yesterday! On the first day of each month, superstitious people say "white rabbits" for luck before speaking out loud. At the beginning of each month, I give Stephanie's teacher $10 for the Friday Lunch Club. I have a meeting on the second Tuesday of every month. A book order form and a newsletter come home once a month from school. There is a monthly meeting of the School Council. At the end of each month, my son Patrick presents a book report, which is based on a novel that he has theoretically been reading over the course of the last 30 days. June is the last month of school. There are no classes during the summer months of July and August. We drive to our cottage in Nova Scotia late in July and don't come home until the middle of August. It is warm on the beach, but we can picture the ice flows that will soon clot the mighty Atlantic Ocean. We shiver at the thought of winter and the way it drags on for six long, cold months from October to March. In April, spring will come again and the snow will give way to rain. It will rain a lot. The black flies and mosquitoes will come out to drink our blood and make us itch. Summer waits for us in the month of May. That is when we plant our flower and vegetable gardens. The hot, hazy, humid weather will stay for July and August when we are on the beach. When we get home, we will swim in my parents' pool to cool our skin and wish for air conditioning so that we could sleep at night. We will complain about the heat instead of the cold. The month of September will arrive and it will grow cool again. Indian Summer will not last. Like autumn, school starts again in September. The leaves change color. It is too cold for shorts in the morning but too hot for long pants in the afternoon. Before we are ready, it is the month of December. We spend this month shopping, decorating and panicking. On January 1, the first day of the new month and the New Year, we will take down our old calendar. There are no more pages, no more months to turn to after December. In its place we will hang a new 12-month calendar and turn to the first page—January—to start the cycle all over again.

Activity 16

Oh, Baby!

*Ask a parent to help you develop a 12-month family birthday list. Try to include as many relatives as possible: your immediate family, grandparents, aunts, uncles and cousins. Tally the number of birthdays that occur in each month. Take these monthly statistics and plot them on a graph (with **Number of Birthdays** on the vertical axis and **Month** on the horizontal axis) to find out which are the most and least popular baby months in your family.*

Example: My Family Birthday List
January: Bet (27th)
February: Derek (14th), Angela (23rd)
March: Connor (6th), Lorraine (8th), Linda (13th), Jono (22nd), Patrick (28th)
April: Grandpa C. (6th), Mary Lou (17th), Bob (19th), Grandpa G. (20th)
May: Jennifer (14th), Linda (15th), Tracey (20th), Bryan (22nd)
June: Grandma C. (6th), Kelley (9th), Meghan (20th)
July: Bryan (7th), Grandma G. (10th), Scott (17th), Graeme (18th), Matt (21st)
August: Beryle (1st), Barb (9th), Cameron (10th), Mattie (12th), Stephanie (13th), Penny (14th), Pat (22nd), Taylor (27th)
September:
October: Michael (20th), Rhianna (22nd)
November: Valerie (26th), Maureen (29th)
December: Paul (6th), Kerri (20)

Month Tallies

January: 1
February: 2
March: 5
April: 4
May: 4
June: 3
July: 5
August: 8
September: 0
October: 2
November: 2
December: 2

Most Popular: August
Least Popular: September

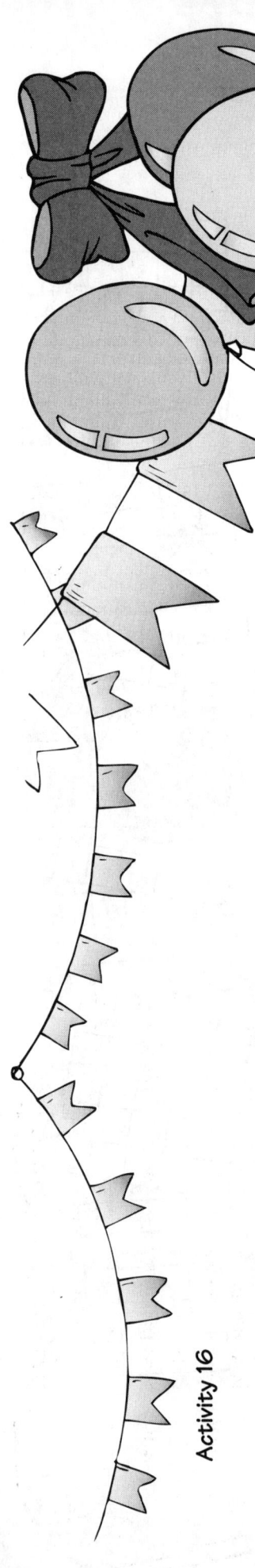

Activity 17

Trip Tracking

Think of a trip you have taken recently, either with your class, with a friend or with your family. Use picture symbols and/or words to order—or sequence—the events that took place on the trip.
(Don't forget to draft your event list first.)

Example: Patrick's Birthday Trip to Northwood

- **12:30:** We arrive at Northwood Buffalo and Exotic Animal Ranch.
- **12:35:** We wander down the hill to see the new grizzly bears.
- **12:50:** We see the four tiny lion cubs at the front gate.
- **12:55:** We pay our admission.
- **1:00:** We sing with Honey the gibbon.
- **1:15:** We visit the three amigos (a trio of adolescent male lions).
- **1:20:** We see the buffalo.
- **1:25:** We are snarled at by a leopard.
- **1:30:** We watch the goats ramming heads.
- **1:45:** We see the llama.
- **1:50:** We hear (and see) the wolves howling.
- **1:55:** We are startled by the sudden flight of a pair of bald eagles.
- **2:00:** We watch the tigers pacing the perimeter of their enclosure.
- **2:10:** We are stunned by the ostrich's grotesque beauty.
- **2:15:** We feed the goats at the other side of their enclosure (more head butting).
- **2:30:** We carry the escaped baby goat in our arms.
- **2:35:** We fall in love with the soft muzzle of the baby donkey.
- **2:45:** The mountain lions and baby tigers stalk and pounce at the kids from behind bars.
- **2:50:** We watch the polar bear perform his "visitor's dance."
- **3:00:** We climb in the van and wave good-bye to our animal friends.

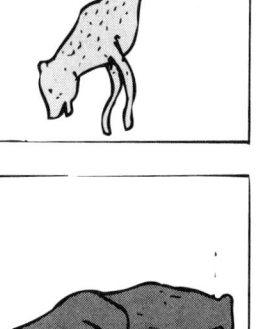
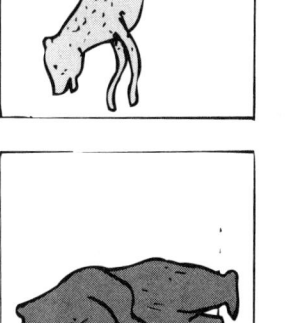
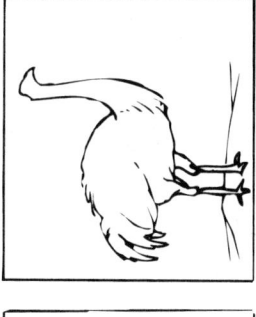
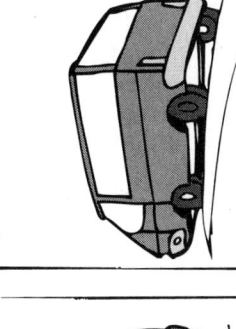
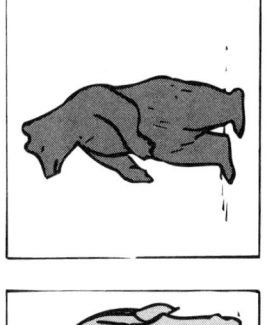
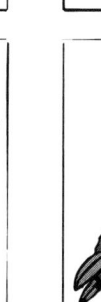
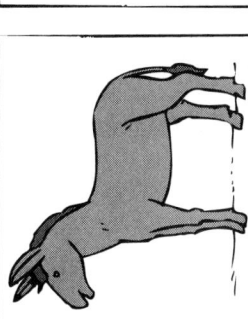

Activity 18

Happy Holidays!

Using dates and pictures, draw a time line that shows the holidays and special events you celebrate every year. (Make sure to draft your event list first.)

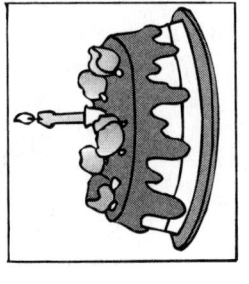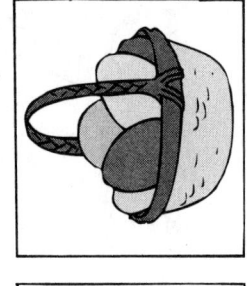
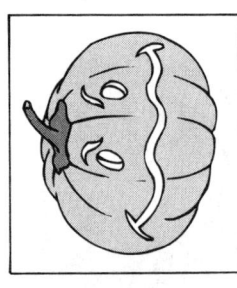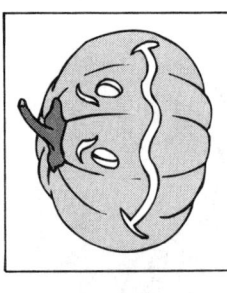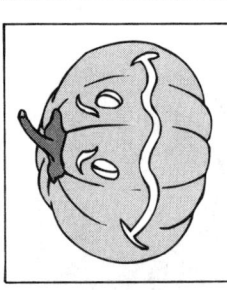
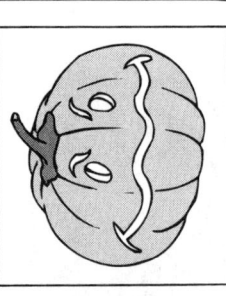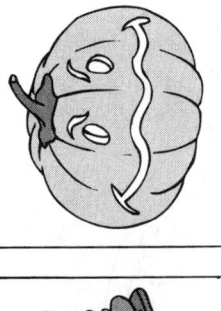

Example: Annual Holiday/Celebration List

January 1:	New Year's Day
February 14:	Valentine's Day
March 22:	Jonathan's birthday
March (mid-month):	Groundhog Day
March 28:	Patrick's birthday
April 1:	April Fools' Day
April (mid-month):	Good Friday/Easter
May (Sunday mid-month):	Mother's Day
May 20:	My birthday
May (Monday around the 20th):	Victoria Day
June (Sunday mid-month):	Father's Day
June (end of month):	Last day of school!
July 1:	Canada Day
August 3:	Our anniversary
August (first Monday):	Civic Holiday
August 9:	Mom's birthday
August 12:	Matthew's birthday
August 13:	Stephanie's birthday
September (first Monday):	Labor Day
September (Sunday mid-month):	Grandparents' Day
October (Monday mid-month):	Thanksgiving Day
October 31:	Halloween
November 11:	Remembrance Day
December 6:	Dad's birthday
December 24:	Christmas Eve
December 25:	Christmas Day
December 26:	Boxing Day
December 31:	New Year's Eve

Activity 19

My Major Milestones

With help from someone who "knew you when," use dates and pictures to construct a time line that shows the major milestones in your life: birth, home from the hospital, first smile, first rollover, first independent sit, first forward crawl, first kiss, first wave bye-bye, first words, first tooth, first hair, first steps, first birthday party, first sentence, first favorite toy, first lost tooth, first day of daycare/school, first vacation, first friend, first pet, first teacher, first broken bone, first sport/activity, first time without training wheels . . . . (Space constraints will force you to be selective in the events that you choose to record. Maybe you'll decide to cover just the first year of your life. Maybe you'll want to make a record of your entire life but just choose the most important or interesting milestones.)

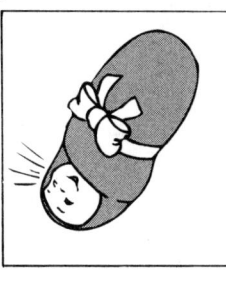
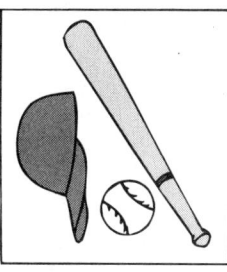
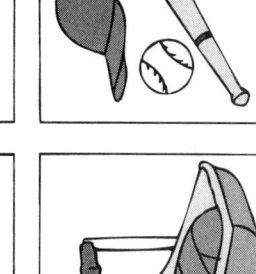
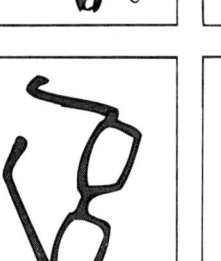
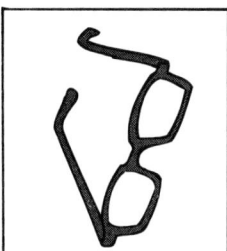

Example: Tracey Schofield's Major Milestones

- **1963:** Tracey is born.
- **1965:** welcomes sibling (Matthew)
- **1968:** starts junior kindergarten
- **1969:** first haircut
- **1970:** first stitches
- **1972:** first dog, Bun Warrior
- **1973:** glasses
- **1974:** major correctional surgery on right foot
- **1975:** first migraine
- **1976:** falls face first on diving board
- **1977:** corrective facial plastic surgery
- **1978:** first summer job and contact lenses
- **1979:** ears pierced and driver's license
- **1980:** dating first serious boyfriend
- **1982:** awarded history scholarship and begins studies in journalism
- **1983:** meets future husband at racetrack and begins studies in English/Zoology
- **1985:** graduates from university with B.A., marries and moves to Ottawa
- **1986:** first full-time job
- **1987:** moves to Arnprior and has first child (Matthew)
- **1988:** starts freelance writing/editing career
- **1990:** has second child (Patrick) and moves to Braeside
- **1991:** has third child (Stephanie)
- **1993:** starts playing women's softball
- **1996:** moves to Whitby
- **1997:** first books published
- **1999:** moves to Seagrave
- **2000:** starts "healthy living" program

Activity 20

Rules Rule

List five important safety rules that you must obey when you are at a public swimming pool, a park or movie theater, in the playground, at recess, on the ice, horseback riding, trick or treating on Halloween . . . . . Why are these rules important?

Notice that the same rule can be written in a negative way—using the word(s) NEVER (or DO NOT)—or in a positive way—using the word(s) ALWAYS (or DO). Write your five rules both ways. Which way do you think is most effective? Do you think kids are more likely to obey "do" or "do not" rules? (It is interesting that the word ALWAYS can be dropped from the sentence and the rule still says and means the same thing. The omission of the word NEVER, however, changes the meaning of the rule comupletely and suggests the opposite of what is intended.)

rule: a standard, principle, regulation, guide or formula for procedure or conduct, as for playing games, solving problems or constructing sentences; established method; accepted usage.

Example:
Our (Negative) Backyard Rules / Our (Positive) Backyard Rules

Never go into the woods alone. / (Always) take a friend with you when you go into the woods.

Never go close to the river. / (Always) stay well back from the river.

Never leave the backyard without telling a parent. / (Always) tell a parent where you are going.

Never throw rocks or swing sticks. / (Always) leave sticks and rocks on the ground where they belong.

Never eat any wild berries, fruits or mushrooms. / (Always) ask a parent before you eat any wild berries, fruits or mushrooms.

Never bother or hurt another living creature. / (Always) respect other living creatures and leave them undisturbed.

Activity 21

House Rules

Make a list of at least 10 rules that apply in your home.
(I've done the first one for you.)
Are you punished if you break one of these rules?
If so, how?

Example: House Rules

1. _You must do your homework before you watch TV._
2. ___
3. ___
4. ___
5. ___
6. ___
7. ___
8. ___
9. ___
10. ___

Punishment: If my kids break this rule, they lose their television privileges for the next day.

Activity 22

School Rules

Make a list of at least 10 school rules.
(I've done the first one for you.)
Choose one of the school rules on your list.
What is the purpose of this rule?
What might happen if your fellow students disregarded it?

Example: School Rules

1. _Don't run in the halls._
2. ___
3. ___
4. ___
5. ___
6. ___
7. ___
8. ___
9. ___
10. ___

Don't run in the halls is an important school safety rule. If everyone started running in the halls, people would be crashing into one another—left, right and center. Books and bags would get knocked out of people's hands and scattered everywhere. Big kids would trample little kids. Teachers and students wouldn't be able to stop at the doorways of their classrooms—they'd get pushed or pulled right on by. It would be only a matter of time before someone got knocked flying into a wall or onto the floor and received a grievous injury.

Activity 23

Out and About

List some of the important safety rules that apply in the community. (I've already done one.) These might include: look all ways before you cross the street, don't talk to strangers, wear a helmet when riding your bike, keep your pet on a leash....

Choose one of the rules on your list and describe how it is intended to keep you safe and why it is important that you obey it.

Example: Community Safety Rules

1. <u>Do not walk into the roadway from between two parked cars.</u>
2. _____
3. _____
4. _____
5. _____
6. _____
7. _____
8. _____
9. _____
10. Do not walk into the roadway from between two parked cars is a rule that is intended to keep you safe by making sure that you are clearly visible to automobile traffic and that automobile traffic is clearly visible to you. When you step out from between two parked cars, motorists might not be able to see you (and you might not be able to see motorists) until the very last second. If you have stepped too far into the roadway, this split second might not be enough to prevent an accident from occurring. Following this safety rule will help to keep you safe by preventing a car from hitting, injuring and possibly killing you. It will also help to keep others safe. If the driver of the car is forced to swerve to avoid you, he or she might hit another car or pedestrian, possibly injuring or killing others. The mental health of the driver is also at stake. A driver who has been involved in an accident of this nature–even if he or she is not responsible for the accident–is at real risk for psychological damage.

Activity 24

Playing by the Rules

Imagine what recreation would be like if there were no rules to tell us how to play a game or a sport. How could you play tag, Monopoly™ or Crazy Eights? What about hockey, baseball or soccer? List at least 10 of the rules for your favorite sport or game. What would happen to that sport or game if you eliminated one of these rules?

Example: Tag
1. The oldest person playing the game is "it."
2. The person who is "it" chases after and tries to touch—or "tag"—another player.
3. When the person who is "it" successfully tags another player, that tagged player becomes "it."
4. The previous "it" returns to the game as a player who can now be tagged.

Let's say we eliminated the third rule. That would mean that the person who started the game as "it" would remain "it" for the entire game. That wouldn't be very fair or very fun.

Activity 25

A World Without Rules

Sometimes parents, teachers and other adults make rules that don't seem fair. Write about one of these rules. Now try to look at it from the rule maker's point of view. Why might a grown-up impose such a rule?

Example: Bedtime
When I was younger, I had to be in bed by 8:30 every night. I could then read for one-half hour. If I did not have my book put away and my light out by 9:00 p.m., I would have to go to bed one half-hour earlier the next night. It didn't seem fair, particularly when I wasn't even tired.

Years later, and looking back from the experienced perspective of a mother, I understand why my parents were so concerned about my bedtime. It is very important that a body is given enough time to rest. It is while kids are sleeping that they do most of their growing and healing during times of illness. It has also been suggested that getting enough sleep is a critical indicator of academic success: kids who are tired are not able to learn as well as those who are well rested. Judging from my own experience, kids who are overtired tend to "act out" more and get into trouble. Without enough sleep, they don't have the energy reserves to deal reasonably and rationally with life's little disappointments. Small problems seem like major disasters and provoke tears and nasty outbursts.

Activity 26

Rule Makers/
Rule Breakers

1. Write a new rule for your home or school. Explain how this rule would benefit the members of your family or fellow students.

2. Think about a rule you have broken. Why did you do it? What happened (or could have happened) as a result?

3. Look in a newspaper. Find an article about someone who has broken a rule. What happened as a result of his or her disobedience? What kind of punishment might society mete out to the rule breaker?

Examples:

1. The "Mean and Clean Rule"
From now on, any family member who is unkind or abusive, physically or verbally, to another member of this family must vacuum one room of the house. This punishment is to be carried out immediately.

This rule would improve the health and welfare of the people living in my household in two ways. When the rule was being obeyed, it would reduce conflict and help to promote a peaceful relationship between members of my family. When the rule was broken, the consequences would ensure a cleaner home environment.

2. Once when I was a teenager, I didn't tell my parents the truth about where I was going. This was a very stupid thing to do. What if something had happened to me? What if I had run into some kind of trouble and couldn't call home for help? My parents would have had no idea where I was. They couldn't have come to my rescue. They wouldn't even have been able to retrace my steps and try to figure out my approximate whereabouts. I got away with breaking the "always tell a parent where you are going" rule, but it could easily have been the kind of disobedience that ended my life. I hope my children are honest with me so that I can help keep them safe.

3. In an effort to improve air quality and reduce smog, the city of Toronto introduced an "anti-idling" by-law aimed at drivers who let their car engines idle and blow noxious exhaust fumes into the air. Drivers who are caught "loitering curbside" with their engines running for more than three minutes face a $130 fine and a stern warning about the hazards of tailpipe pollution. Yesterday, one enforcement team handed out six tickets to motorists who were caught disregarding the anti-idling law.

The Globe and Mail, June 5, 2000

Activity 27

Cool Rules

Make a list of 10 rules for: your pet, your best friend, your parents, your siblings, your teacher, your hair, your desk, your homework, your personal servant . . . .

Example: 10 Rules for My Houseplants
1. You must grow.
2. You must be hardy, tolerant and drought resistant.
3. Your leaves must not turn brown at the tips.
4. You must blossom and bloom year-round.
5. You must stay upright and healthy despite frequent feline attacks.
6. You must not let any dirt escape from your pot onto the carpet.
7. You must not be sensitive to changes in temperature.
8. You must learn to live without vitamins.
9. You must never require repotting.
10. You must not be poisonous if a child accidentally eats one of your leaves.

Activity 28

I Have My Rights

Make a list of your rights as a member of your country, your community, your family, your church, your school, your class, your team, your club, your group of friends . . . .

Example: As a writer . . . .
I have the right to freedom of expression.
I have the right to commit my thoughts and experiences to paper.
I have the right to make public my opinions and ideas.
I have the right to disclose personal and confidential information about myself.
I have the right to call my words and my works my own.
I have the right to claim intellectual ownership of the materials I have written.
I have the right to negotiate a contract with the publisher of my choice.
I have the right to decline publication of my intellectual property.
I have the right to quote freely from my own printed works.
I have the right to obtain copies of my own published material.
I have the right to promote my publications in the media and to society at large.
I have the right to teach courses based on the materials I have developed.
I have the right to call myself a published author.

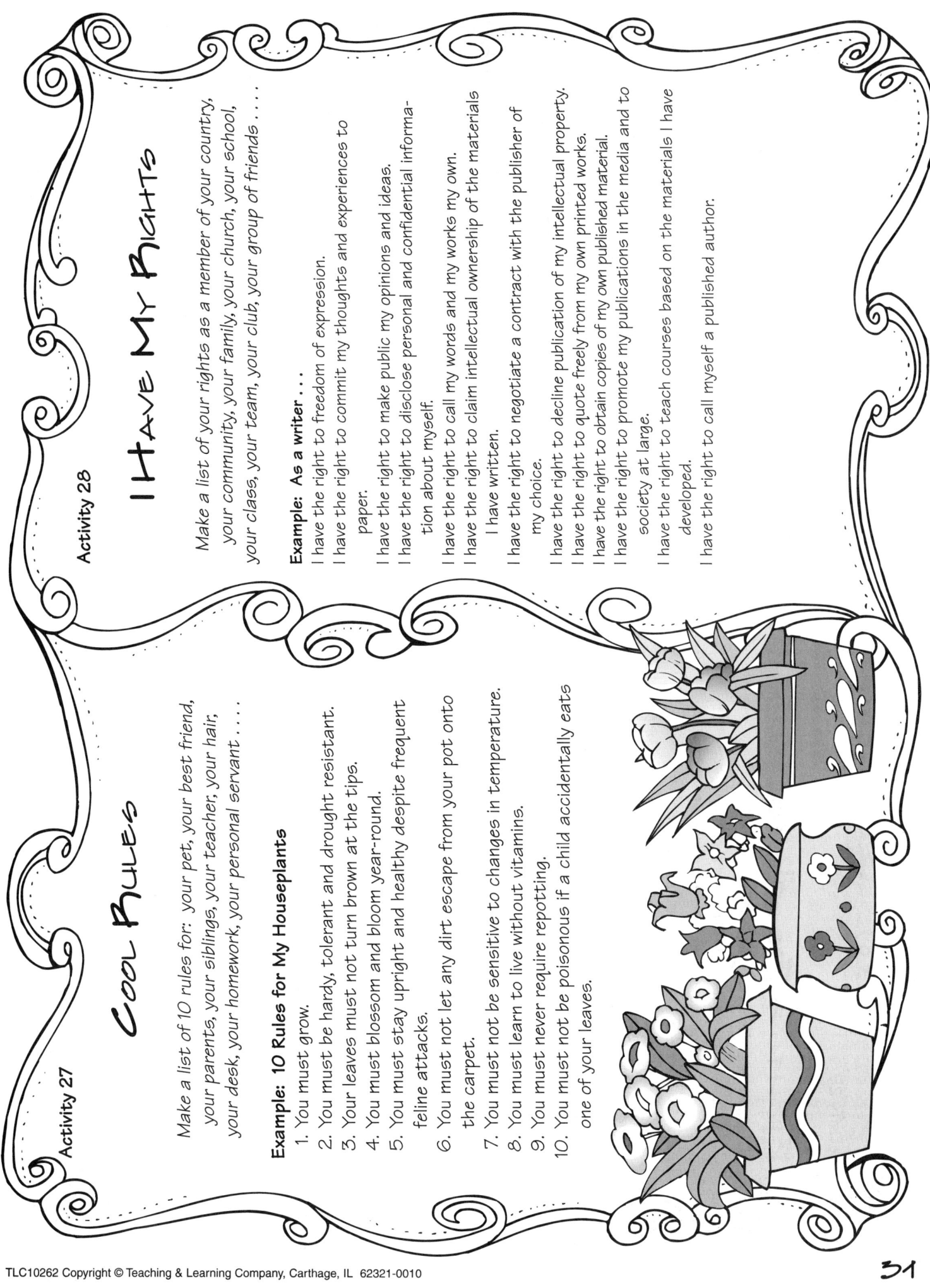

Activity 29

Rights = Responsibilities

Rights and responsibilities are a package deal. You cannot have one without the other. For every right that you enjoy, there are associated responsibilities. Think of one of your rights. What responsibilities go hand in hand with that right?

responsibility: the state of being answerable or accountable, legally or morally, as for an obligation, duty, trust or debt; a duty, charge or obligation

Example: My Right and My Responsibility

Right: Freedom of speech
Responsibility: To refrain from hurting another person with my words.

Although I am allowed to speak (and write) freely of my thoughts, ideas and opinions, I must not say or write things that might injure others. Specifically I am not to abuse this right to freedom of speech by maliciously uttering and circulating lies and false reports that could damage the reputation of another person (slander) or by writing or publishing mean, unjustified statements that are designed to defame the character of another person (libel).

Activity 30

Mighty Obliged

Describe your responsibilities as a member of your family or a student in your class or your school.

Example: My Responsibilities as a Mother

As a mother, I am responsible for (among other things):

- providing nutritious meals for my children
- ensuring that my children are sufficiently hydrated (have access to fluids)
- giving my children an adequate place to live
- making sure that my children are clean and healthy
- seeking medical attention and administering medications when my children are ill
- providing my children with clothes to wear that will protect them from the elements
- keeping my children safe by making them aware of potential dangers
- protecting my children from neglect and abuse
- making my children feel secure in their home and in my love for them
- ensuring that my children attend school
- helping my children with their homework
- providing my children with opportunities for socialization and recreation
- ensuring that my children are physically and intellectually challenged
- offering emotional support, empathy, sympathy and understanding to my children
- establishing rules and structure in our home
- educating my children about and ensuring they conform to societal norms
- disciplining my children when they are disobedient
- limiting the quantity/monitoring the quality of the entertainment enjoyed by my children
- providing my children with cultural experiences
- exposing my children to the arts
- giving my children the tools they need to explore and master their environment
- helping my children to achieve their fullest potential as independent human beings and contributing members of society

TLC10262 Copyright © Teaching & Learning Company, Carthage, IL 62321-0010

33

Activity 31

Behaving Responsibly

What if an adult made you responsible for feeding the classroom pet, taking the attendance to the school office in the morning, locking the door behind you, taking care of your younger brother or sister, making your lunch, putting your dirty clothes in the laundry basket . . . ? What might happen if you refused this responsibility or didn't take it seriously?

Example 1: Neglecting My Responsibilities

If I did not take seriously my responsibility for feeding my children and did not provide them with a balanced diet, they might develop diseases and deficiencies. Their skin and teeth might deteriorate. They might suffer from stomach and bowel disorders. They would not have the energy required to attend school and learn new things. They would not have the strength for physical activity or recreation. If left alone to meet their nutritional needs, they might make unhealthy food choices or neglect meals altogether and wind up ill or dangerously over- or underweight. Taken to the extreme, if I did not ensure that food was readily available to my children, they might weaken to the point of unconsciousness and eventually even starve to death.

Choose one of your responsibilities as a member of your family, class, church, sports team, club, community group, neighborhood . . . Describe this responsibility. Write about what might happen if you decided to neglect one aspect of this responsibility.

Example 2: The Pitcher

As a pitcher for a women's softball team, my responsibilities include: pitching the ball, throwing strikes, covering home plate when a runner is on third base, catching pop flies and fielding ground balls in my area of the diamond, communicating with the back-catcher regarding the pitches to be thrown, listening to my coach, being aware of any runners on base, making sure that my teammates are ready before I pitch the ball, and not striking any batters with my pitches. If I decided not to take responsibility for throwing strikes—if I decided to throw the ball over my shoulder or into the stands instead of across the plate in the strike zone—I would make it impossible for my team to remain competitive. I would walk batter after batter and walk in run after run. Eventually my coach would pull me out of the game and replace me with another pitcher, but I might have placed my teammates at such a disadvantage that no amount of effort could salvage the game. As a member of a sporting team, it is my responsibility to try my very best on behalf of myself, my teammates and our fans. To do otherwise is to neglect my responsibilities as a team player.

TLC10262 Copyright © Teaching & Learning Company, Carthage, IL 62321-0010

Activity 32

It's Not My Job

Choose one of the scenarios below (or make up your own) and describe what would happen if these people decided to shirk their responsibility to you and to society.

Example: What would happen if school bus drivers no longer drove school buses?

A lot of kids would have no way of getting to school. They couldn't walk. The distance and danger would be too great. For parents who work, the school bus is the only feasible means of transportation for their children. Even for families that might have the opportunity to drive their kids to school, it would be a disaster. Making this kind of trip twice each school day would cost a lot of money in gas, and could add hundreds of miles of annual wear and tear to their vehicles. With so many more vehicles on the road every morning and afternoon, air pollution would increase dramatically. If buses were driven by inexperienced people or people who were not properly trained and licensed to commandeer such big vehicles and cope with the distraction of dozens of talking, yelling, fighting kids, the number of road accidents would surely escalate. Driving a school bus is an enormous responsibility, and it takes a very special kind of person to do this work. If bus drivers were to shirk their responsibilities or just quit en masse, school-aged children, their families and society at large would be in serious trouble.

What would happen if . . .

- . . . your parents decided they were no longer responsible for your welfare?
- . . . doctors decided your health was not their concern?
- . . . police and firefighters refused to accept responsibility for your safety?
- . . . soldiers no longer cared about your protection and your freedom?
- . . . teachers ceased to be responsible for your education?
- . . . garbage collectors no longer wanted to burden themselves with your trash?
- . . . farmers felt that producing milk was not their responsibility?
- . . . pilots couldn't be bothered flying airplanes?
- . . . car salespeople felt that selling motor vehicles was too much trouble?

What would happen to society if no one accepted responsibility for anything?

Activity 33

Show a Little Respect

By respecting the rights of others, we are, in a way, taking responsibility for their happiness, health and well-being. This is part of being a considerate and contributing member of society.

Example: Keeping your walkway free of ice and snow during the winter months.

By shoveling and deicing my walkway, I am respecting the inalienable and personal right to protection that is enjoyed by all people. By making sure that others do not slip and fall and injure themselves on my walkway, I am thereby taking responsibility for and respecting their right to safety.

Explain how one of the following demonstrates responsible behavior and respect for the rights of others:

- being polite and courteous (holding the door for others, saying "please" and "thank you," listening when spoken to . . . .)
- allowing others their personal space
- cooperating, sharing (of library books, school supplies, playground equipment, etc.)
- keeping the school yard clean
- staying out of your brother's room
- keeping off the grass
- keeping a pair of clean shoes at school for indoor use
- saying "excuse me" before interrupting a conversation
- putting your wrappers in a trash can
- moving over to let someone else pass you on the sidewalk
- using the bell on your bike to announce your presence to pedestrians
- keeping your pet on a leash or in your own backyard
- "stooping and scooping" (cleaning up after your dog)
- composting and recycling

Think of five additional examples of respectful behavior.

Activity 34

Wronged Rights

How do things like...

- reading someone else's diary
- talking back to your teachers or parents
- touching things that don't belong to you
- feeding animals at the zoo
- breaking branches off a neighbor's tree
- looking in someone's purse or backpack
- leaving toys on the stairs
- writing on bathroom walls
- using foul language in public
- bullying younger children
- laughing at the mistakes of others
- criminal behaviors such as littering, loitering, stealing, vandalizing and causing bodily harm

...infringe on the rights of others? Choose one and explain.

Think of at least five more examples of behaviors or actions that are disrespectful of the rights of others and therefore contrary to our civic responsibilities.

Example: Interrupting or Talking Out During Class

When I interrupt or talk out during class, I am infringing on the rights of my teachers and fellow students. My fellow students have the right to attend classes in a supportive environment that allows them to listen and to learn from their instructors without distraction. Similarly, my teachers have the right to impart knowledge to the students in their classes in the same environment and to gain the respect–and attention–of those students. Teachers and students have the right to a quiet, comfortable atmosphere that is conducive to productive instruction and learning.

Activity 35

Rightful Restoration

Think of one activity or behavior that compromises the rights of others. Explain the effects of this activity or behavior. Try to think of at least five corrective measures that could be taken to restore the rights wronged by this activity or behavior.

Example: Bullying at School
Bullies compromise their victims' rights to safety, security and happiness.

To restore these rights, we might . . .
- enforce a "zero tolerance" policy for bullying at school
- establish a "watchdog program" for anonymous reporting of bullying incidents to people in positions of authority
- make conflict resolution and anger management counseling mandatory for "convicted" bullies
- teach victims acceptable methods of self-defense and strategies that will help them stand up for their rights
- have bullies and former victims work together on a cooperative project in a constructive and supportive environment

No Bullies

Activity 36

Changing the Rules

When circumstances change, rules sometimes have to change, too. Think of the rules that apply to your life now and describe how these might have to change as the result of a new baby, a new pet, a new grade, a new home, a new school, a new parent, a new coach, a new teacher, a new danger . . . . .

Example: Construction begins on a new housing development at the foot of your street

In the past, you might have been able to play in the field at the foot of your street. Now, you will have to stay clear of the area. You might have been able to ride your bike up and down the length of your street, but construction traffic and the dangers associated with heavy machinery and the limited visibility of the truck drivers make it unsafe. You might have to stop 10 houses before the end of your street and turn around. You might not be able to ride your skateboard on the road because of the dirt and gravel left behind by the dump trucks. You might have to go the long way, rather than cut through the field to get to school or to your best friend's house. You might not be able to play street hockey for a while. You might have to take a different route to walk your dog.

Activity 37

Bask in the Glory or Suffer the Consequences?

*Would you sooner receive praise or punishment?
Would you rather be a part of society or apart from it?
Think of one example and describe what might happen if . . .*
*a. you follow the rules, fulfill your responsibilities,
respect the rights of others*
*b. you break the rules, neglect your responsibilities,
infringe on the rights of others.*

Example: Taking care of your little brother while your mother makes dinner.

a. If you follow the rules, fulfill your responsibilities and respect the rights of others by taking good care of your little brother—by entertaining your little brother and keeping him occupied, by making sure he plays and stays safe, by focusing on the task at hand and not allowing your attention to stray to other things that might be more interesting (like television)—your mother will be very grateful for your help and the maturity you have shown in carrying out your responsibilities. She might think about hiring you to baby-sit at another time. She might reward you with praise or grant you a special privilege. She might empower you to do other things—fun things—that can be enjoyed only by people who are capable of handling the level of responsibility associated with greater freedom (staying home alone, going to a movie with friends, etc.).

b. On the other hand, if you break the rules, neglect your responsibilities and infringe on the rights of others—by failing to properly supervise your baby brother; by interrupting, distracting and upsetting your mother; or by allowing your little brother to endanger or hurt himself—you will probably be reprimanded or punished. Your mother will be angry and unlikely to go out of her way for you in the near future. She will be reluctant to grant you any special privileges, and she certainly won't think about offering to pay you to do a job that you are clearly not ready, willing or able to do.

Activity 38

Different Strokes for Different Folks

Different sets of rules apply to different groups of people. Rules can be different for someone living around the world and someone living around the corner. Rules vary according to such things as age, geographic location, race, religion, culture, weather, season, school, team, teacher, parent, child. . . .

List 10 rules that you live by and describe how these things might be different for someone who lives differently than you.

a. Why are the two sets of rules different?

b. What is different about the two groups of people the rules were designed to protect and direct?

Example:

Rules That Apply to Big Brother Matthew	Rules That Apply to Baby Sister Stephanie
Bedtime is 8:30 p.m.	Bedtime is 7:30 p.m.
Can ride bike around the block	Can ride her tricycle on the driveway
Can watch one hour of TV after school	Can watch many hours of TV all day
Can have three friends over to play	Can have one friend over to play
Can have two cookies for dessert	Can have one cookie for dessert
Must clean place after dinner	Does not have to clean place after dinner
Can watch scary movies	Cannot watch scary movies
Can play by himself in the park	Has to go to the park with an adult
Can take a shower alone	Must have a supervised bath
Can walk to school with friends	Must walk to school with Mom or Dad

The rules are different because Matthew and Stephanie are different ages. Stephanie is much younger and cannot be given as much responsibility and freedom as her brother. Matthew is older, has a better understanding of the way the world works, and can take pretty good care of himself. In some ways, the rules seem to favor Stephanie. She can watch TV all day long and does not have to clear her place at dinner. (This is because she does not yet attend school and watches a lot of educational television and because she does not have the coordination to carry her dinner dishes to the sink.) In other ways, they work better for Matthew: he can stay up until 8:30 and play at the park by himself. (Stephanie needs more sleep than Matthew so her bedtime is one hour earlier. She cannot yet take responsibility for her own safety so must have an adult to supervise her at the playground.) As Matthew and Stephanie get older, the rules that govern their activities will change. Eventually, the two might live under the same set of rules.

Traditions and Celebrations

In this section, students identify their family origins, record significant personal, family and community events and discuss the impact of culture and heritage on their everyday lives. They examine the traditions and special celebrations that reinforce their cultural heritage and develop an understanding of and appreciation for cultural diversity. Specifically, they . . .

- develop an understanding of the term culture (Activities 39-40)
- demonstrate an understanding that traditions are passed down from parents and grandparents (Activities 41-47)
- identify ways in which heritage passes from generation to generation (Activities 48-55)
- demonstrate an understanding that communities may be made up of many cultures (Activity 56)
- identify the significant features of various cultures and the cultural origins of their classmates (Activity 57)
- identify community celebrations that reflect their own heritage and cultural identity (Activity 58)
- describe the contributions each family makes to the community and identify the special contributions of various cultures (Activity 59)

Activity 39

Cultural Creatures

Human beings are creatures of culture. We are the sum total of all that our parents and their parents and the long line of parents that came before them have attained and achieved. Culture is a learned behavior, passed down through generations, and includes such things as belief systems, languages and stories, traditions, social relationships, institutions and organizations, agriculture, economics, music, art and material goods (food, clothing, buildings, tools and machines). While we share many cultural characteristics with people of the same race, ethnic background and geographical location, subtle differences in personal experience and family history give each one of us a unique cultural heritage.

As an analogy, consider humankind's best friend, the dog. While all domestic dogs are Canids (directly related to the wolf), each breed of dog is recognized and bred for specific characteristics. Within that breed each dog has its own unique personality which reflects both its parentage and its life experience. Our last dog, Bob, was a Labrador Retriever. He had the "broad skull, pronounced brow, wide nose, powerful neck, barrel-shaped ribcage and distinctive otter-like tail" of all Labradors. He shared a common heritage with other members of his breed: Labrador Retrievers originated in Newfoundland, Canada, in the 1800s and were used to help fishermen haul their nets ashore. Like all Labs, Bob was "responsive and friendly."

But he did not have the work ethic or easy confidence of most Labradors. He was lazy and timid. And because of these characteristics, he failed guide dog school. Also, somewhere in the midst of all his breeding and training, something happened to inhibit the development of his friendly nature. While he was as gentle as a lamb, he did not like to be touched. And this was definitely unLab-like.

In human terms, Bob shared many of the cultural (physical and social) characteristics of his race, yet he was markedly different. Did he inherit these off-breed traits from his mother or father? Was mother Sadie standoffish or father Duke lazy? Or were these peculiarities acquired during his handling as a puppy or rigorous training as an adolescent? Whatever the answers, we know that Bob the Dog was a product of his wolf ancestry (Canid), his breed (Labrador Retriever), his parents (Sadie and Duke and their dispositions) and his upbringing and life experience (guide dog-in-training to household pet).

Just as I am a product of my human ancestry (Homo sapien), my race (white, Anglo-Saxon protestant), my parents (Barb and Paul and their associated beliefs, traditions and peculiarities) and my own upbringing and personal experience (child/young adult of the late 1900s to mother/professional in the early 21st century).

Cultural Creatures continued

My family is very much like the family next door. But it is also very different.

Think about your next-door neighbors.

How are your families alike? How are they different? How might these similarities and differences be the result of cultural heritage?

Example: The Coverts and the Hopewells

I grew up in a semi-detached house. Although our neighbors were very much like us in many ways—they were a two-parent family of two children; they had a car, a camper and a vegetable garden; their kids attended the same schools as we did; etc.–they were also very different.

Our decorating tastes were dramatically different, for example. The Hopewell's house was dark, cluttered with personal mementos and reflective of the 60s in terms of color and furnishings. Our house was bright, spartan and had been largely redecorated with each passing decade.

The Hopewells were curious about what went on in our house. They noticed our comings and goings and commented on our activities. We were intensely private people. We kept pretty much to ourselves and didn't become involved in the daily business of our neighbors.

The Hopewell's spent holidays and summers in the United Kingdom. We stayed at home with family at Christmas time and travelled Canada on our holidays.

The Hopewells spent a lot of time in the garden and were always expanding their flower beds. We converted our flower garden to grass because we wanted more space to play.

Mrs. Hopewell, now a widow, loves suburban life and the comfort and convenience of local amenities, reliable neighbors and old friends. She will probably remain in her small house for the rest of her days. My family members moved to the country to enjoy the open spaces and private places that rural living has to offer as soon as possible.

The fact that our neighbors came from England and my parents were Torontonions could account for many of the differences in our family ways. Emigration forced the Hopewells to find companionship outside of their extended family unit, while we were able to cling to one another and to our nearby relatives. As well, our two families had a very different sense of community. To the Hopewells, who grew up in a small British town, neighborly behavior involved an intimate awareness of lives of those nearby. To my parents, who grew up in the heart of a city, it was most neighborly to leave each family unto its own. The fact that the Hopewells were 15 years older than my parents and grew up under very different political and social circumstances–the war years–could also account for some of the differences between the two houses.

43

Activity 40

A Horse of a Different Color

Think of an animal or pet that you have owned or one that you have read about.
How does this creature conform to the recognized characteristics of its species or particular breed? How does it differ?
What might account for these similarities and differences?

Example: Hammy the Hamster
My husband and I had a teddy bear hamster when we were first married that was more like a dog than a rodent. She looked like a hamster. She smelled like a hamster. She stuffed her cheek pouches full of seeds like a hamster. But her personality was not that of your average pet store hamster. We would let Hammy out of her cage to wander our two-bedroom apartment freely. She would zip around for hours, hiding here, hiding there, but as soon as we called her name, she would come running out from wherever she was and over to our feet to be scooped up and popped back into her cage. Once, she ran up under a cupboard and into the plumbing space behind our bathroom sink. We thought she was a goner and that she would have disappeared into the bowels of the apartment building forever. But when I put my mouth to the little hole and called her name, out she scrambled. In all my years, I have never heard of another hamster that knew its name and would come faithfully when called. Hamsters are nocturnal creatures and despise being disturbed. They often bite and draw blood if they are surprised or pestered. Hammy seemed to be awake when we were awake and never, ever put her teeth to our flesh. Perhaps it was because she had survived the constant physical abuse of her sibling. Her sister bit her continuously. During one particularly aggressive attack, she tore a chunk of flesh out of Hammy's side that was the size of a quarter. Since small rodents are so susceptible to infection, we thought for certain that Hammy's wound would fester and she would die. But she healed, and a few weeks later, we found her sister dead beneath the wheel in their cage. Was Hammy responsible? Was she so overjoyed at being free of her tormentor that she decided to live life to its fullest? Did she credit us with her sister's death and therefore repay her debt of gratitude with good behavior? Whatever the reasons behind our hamster's altered personality, we were thankful and very sad when she died.

Activity 41

Festive Traditions

A tradition is something–information, opinions, doctrines, practices, etc.–that is "handed down" through successive generations, as from a parent to a child (or a grandparent to a grandchild).

Describe one of your favorite festive or celebratory family traditions (think of religious holidays, birthdays and civic holidays).

Where and with whom did this tradition originate? (Remember: the way you celebrate today might influence the way you celebrate in the future when you have a family of your own.)

tradition: the transmission of knowledge, opinions, doctrines, customs, practices, etc., from generation to generation, originally by word of mouth and by example

Example: 'Twas the Night Before Christmas
On Christmas Eve, just before bed, my family always gathered together to read "Twas the Night Before Christmas." My mom read the story to my brother and me when we were little. Later, when I had learned to read, I read the story to my family. Finally, when my brother was able to join in, we read the story together, alternating pages. (Once, I purposely changed the words according to a joke I had heard: "Twas the night before Christmas when all through the house not a creature was stirring–no spoons. (It was supposed to be not even a mouse.) Boy, did I get in trouble! It was as if I had committed a crime. And I guess, in a way, I had. I had broken and ridiculed a treasured family tradition. I never did that again, but I have never forgotten the incident either.) We always read from the same volume. It had been my mother's when she was a little girl. It was a large, shaped book with a picture of Santa on the front. His red suit was made of a velvety fabric that had been worn by touching through the years and existed only in patches. I still have the book. The cover has been separated from the rest of the pages, but I now read it to my children on Christmas Eve. Over the years I have accumulated other versions of this Christmas favorite, and I read them all to my children over and over again during the month of December. I know the poem by heart. But it is my mother's book with the crushed velvet Santa that comes out on Christmas Eve. And it is that book that my children will remember–and read–when they are grown.

Activity 42

Family Favorites

Recipes are often passed down through the generations. Write down the ingredients and directions for your favorite family recipe. With what family member did this recipe originate?

Example: Dat's (sic)* Oatmeal Cookies

Ingredients
½ lb. butter
1 c. white sugar
½ c. brown sugar
1 egg
1 tsp. vanilla
1½ c. flour
1 tsp. baking soda
1 tsp. baking powder
1½ c. rolled oats
¾ c. coconut

Directions
Soften the butter. Cream the butter and sugars. Add the egg and vanilla and mix well. In a separate bowl, sift together the flour, baking soda and baking powder. Mix the flour mixture into the butter mixture. Add the rolled oats and coconut. Mix. Drop batter by rounded teaspoon onto an ungreased baking sheet. Bake for 12 minutes at 325°F or until cookies flatten and turn a golden brown.

As far as we know, this recipe originated with my great-grandmother, but it could date back even further.

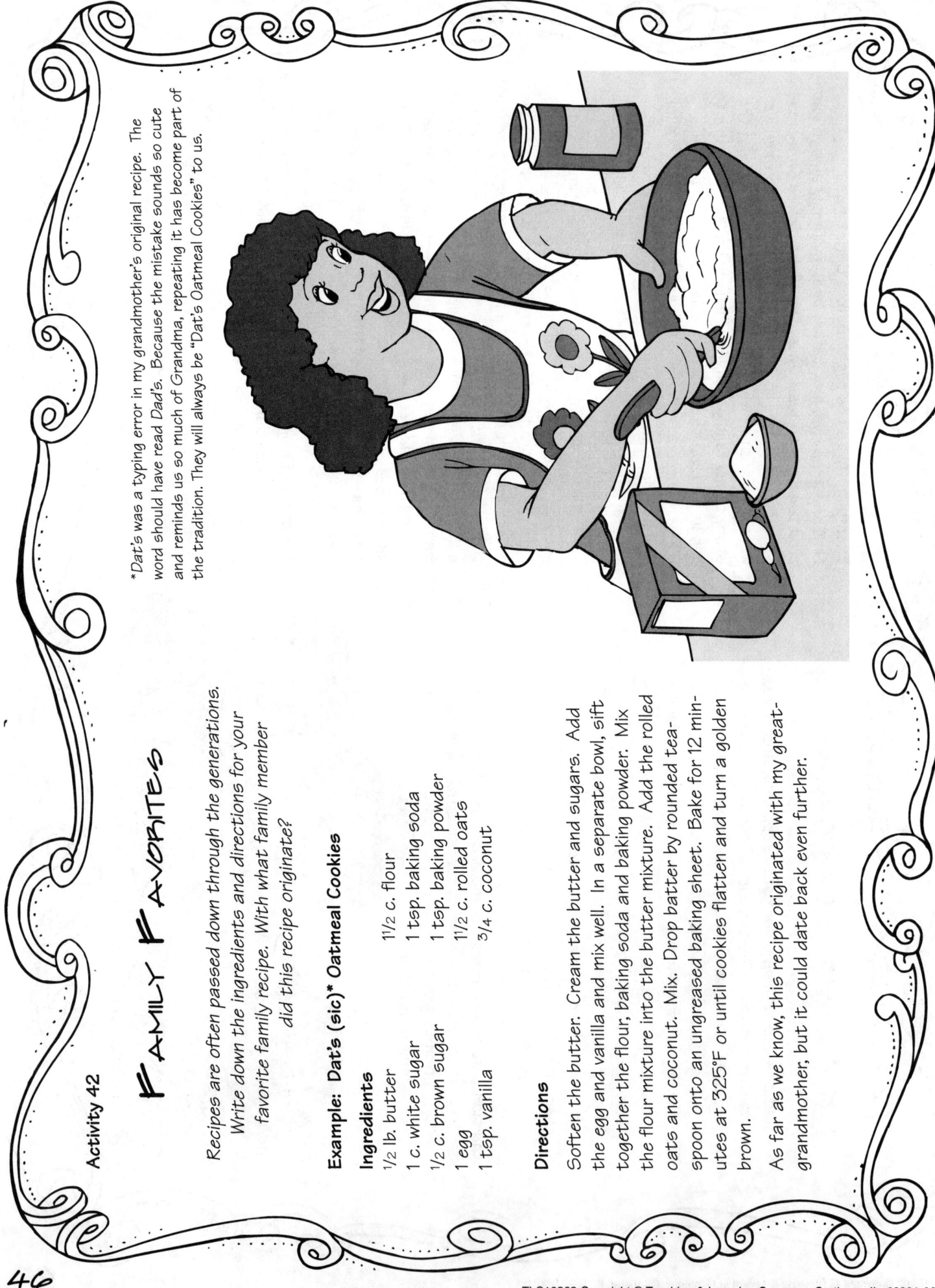

*Dat's was a typing error in my grandmother's original recipe. The word should have read Dad's. Because the mistake sounds so cute and reminds us so much of Grandma, repeating it has become part of the tradition. They will always be "Dat's Oatmeal Cookies" to us.

Activity 43

Treasured Traditions

A tradition can also be a certain way of doing things: the way we prepare and present foods and the kind of foods we eat, our bedtime routines, the way we reward and discipline our children, the kind of pets we keep, the way we spend our holidays and summer vacations, the kind of books we read, the crafts we do, what we do for rest and relaxation . . . .

1. Describe one of your favorite family traditions: something that your parents (or grandparents) do for you that you will definitely do for your children.
2. Describe a quirky family tradition: something that your parents (or grandparents) do, and thus that you do without really understanding why you do it.

Example 1: Back-to-School Shopping

When I was little, my mother always took my brother and me "back-to-school" shopping during the last week of summer vacation. At the mall near our house, we were allowed to buy one new outfit for school: a pair of pants and a T-shirt or sweatshirt. If we were in need, we would get a new pair of sneakers, too. Then we would go and buy our school supplies: a 24-pack of crayons with all those glorious, multicolored, perfectly sharpened tips; a pack of loose-leaf lined binder paper; a ruler; a glue stick; an eraser; a pen; and a couple of pencils. I always looked forward to that day. Even when my stomach was tying itself in knots at the thought of a new grade, a new teacher and a new bunch of kids, my nervous tension would give way to joyful anticipation as Labor Day and our end-of-summer shopping excursion approached. Today, I keep this tradition alive with my kids. I think it eases their back-to-school blues just as it did mine and gives them something special to look forward to as they say good-bye to another summer vacation.

Example 2: The Ham Sham

I once heard a story about a woman who always cut off the end of a ham before putting it in the roasting pan. When people asked her why she did this, she couldn't give them a logical explanation. As a child, she had watched her mother do the same and she simply adopted the practice. (Subconsciously she assumed that there was some flavorful or healthful reason behind this "traditional" activity.) After being asked the "why" question dozens of times, she finally turned it over to her mother. "Why do you always cut off the end of the ham?" she asked. Her mother replied, "because it won't fit in the roasting pan otherwise."

Example 3: The Core War

My mother has always cut the hull out of the center of a strawberry. Although I have no idea why she does this (I assume that the core is fibrous and doesn't taste that great) I do it because she does—even though my mimicry adds hours to the time it takes to make strawberry jam! I have never met anyone else who hulls their strawberries (most people think I am just plain silly for doing it), but I would never dream of omitting this time-consuming traditional step. As far as my mother and I are concerned, hulling is the only way to prepare a strawberry.

47

Activity 44

Breaking with Tradition

What is one family tradition you will do away with when you grow up? What tradition will you begin in its place?

Example: The Dawning of a New Year

When I was little, my parents spent New Year's Eve away from home and out with their friends. My brother and I rang in the New Year with a baby-sitter. As a result, the annual festivities had no real significance for me. When I got married, I celebrated with a glass of soda at midnight and a kiss from my husband. Now that I have kids of my own, I am going to start my own family tradition. Instead of going out and leaving my kids at home, I will either celebrate at home with them or take them with me to sing a chorus of "Auld Lang Syne" with our friends and their kids.

Activity 45

Family Name Game

Some families pass names down through the generations.
1. *Are there any traditional names in your family?*
2. *If you could select one of the names of your ancestors for your own middle name, which would you choose?*

Example 1: Margaret, Ann, Gordon and Maynard

Margaret is a name that my mother's family has passed down. My great-grandmother's name was Margaret, my mother's cousin was Marguerite (a version of Margaret) and my maternal aunt's middle name is Margaret. My grandmother started the "Ann" tradition with my mom, Barbara Ann. Mom and her sister followed suit with Tracey Ann (me) and Patricia Ann (my cousin). To maintain some of her family heritage, my mom chose "Gordon" for my brother's middle name (her maiden name) and I have started a tradition of my own. Like my mother, I wanted to preserve some of my family's heritage after taking my husband's name in marriage. My daughter's middle name is Maynard, which was my maternal grandmother's maiden name.

Example 2: Family Names

If I were to choose a new middle name for myself, I would favor a family name: Maynard or Traynor or Offen or Owen.

Activity 46

Story Savers

One way of keeping family history and traditions alive is through storytelling. Transcribe one infamous family story that you will want to pass on to your children.

Example: The Ballad of the Frog and the Gall Bladder
My family used to spend many summer weekends at a cottage on Georgian Bay. During the evenings we would sit around a campfire and sing songs. One of our favorites was "Down by the Bay." On one celebrated occasion when I was very young, my slightly older (and poetically challenged) cousin had joined us for the weekend. When the time came for her to make a rhyme (such as, "Did you ever see a cat wearing a hat?") she cried out, "Did you ever see a frog having its gall bladder removed?" Although Kelley turned 40 this year, she has never lived down that historic moment.

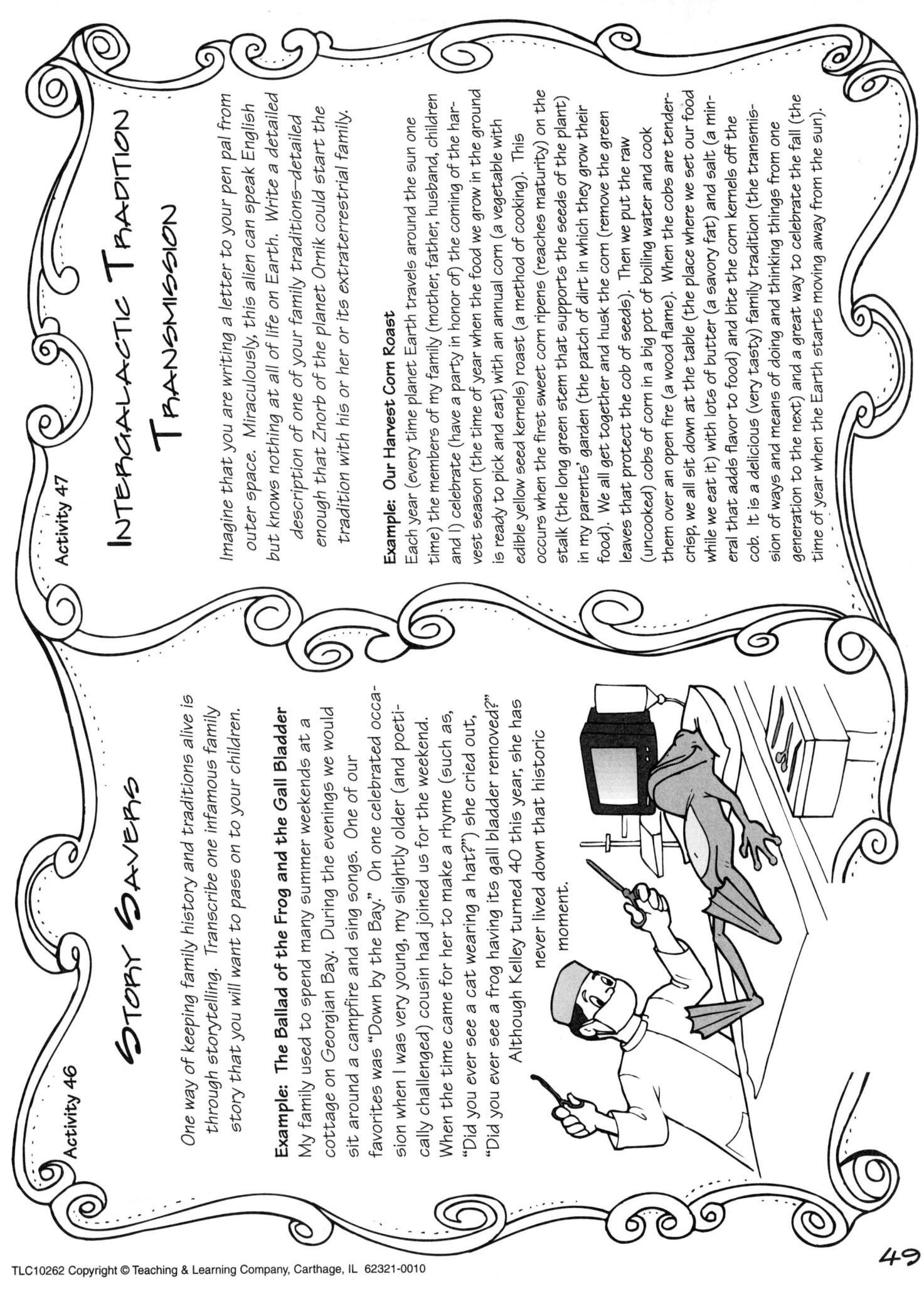

Activity 47

Intergalactic Tradition Transmission

Imagine that you are writing a letter to your pen pal from outer space. Miraculously, this alien can speak English but knows nothing at all of life on Earth. Write a detailed description of one of your family traditions—detailed enough that Znorb of the planet Ornik could start the tradition with his or her or its extraterrestrial family.

Example: Our Harvest Corn Roast
Each year (every time planet Earth travels around the sun one time) the members of my family (mother, father, husband, children and I) celebrate (have a party in honor of) the coming of the harvest season (the time of year when the food we grow in the ground is ready to pick and eat) with an annual corn (a vegetable with edible yellow seed kernels) roast (a method of cooking). This occurs when the first sweet corn ripens (reaches maturity) on the stalk (the long green stem that supports the seeds of the plant) in my parents' garden (the patch of dirt in which they grow their food). We all get together and husk the corn (remove the green leaves that protect the cob of seeds). Then we put the raw (uncooked) cobs of corn in a big pot of boiling water and cook them over an open fire (a wood flame). When the cobs are tender-crisp, we all sit down at the table (the place where we set our food while we eat it) with lots of butter (a savory fat) and salt (a mineral that adds flavor to food) and bite the corn kernels off the cob. It is a delicious (very tasty) family tradition (the transmission of ways and means of doing and thinking things from one generation to the next) and a great way to celebrate the fall (the time of year when the Earth starts moving away from the sun).

Activity 48
Hunting for Heritage

Heritage is anything that passes by descent—material possessions and personal qualities alike. Ask a parent to tell you about something special that one of your grandparents did or owned. Is there something that has been in your family for generations: a property, a piece of jewelry, an incredible story . . . ?

heritage: property that is or can be inherited; an inherited quality or characteristic; any condition or culture which is allotted or handed down to one, as by ancestors

Example: My Grandmother's Piano

When she was a young girl, my grandmother was given a beautiful upright piano. After she died, the piano passed to my father. He did not play, but I did. When I married and bought a house of my own, Dad took that ancient piano apart and moved it into the living room of my new home 400 miles away. We have moved it three times now. It is screwed together in places. The ivory has chipped off many of the keys. The pedals do not work. The low, low and high, high notes are sour. But I still play every now and then and savor the sweet tones. I hope that one of my children will inherit the musical gift that runs in my family so that my grandmother's memory will be enjoyed and sustained for another generation.

Activity 49
Family "Hair"looms

Some families pass personal treasures that have sentimental and/or monetary value down through the ages. These are called heirlooms. For example, you might one day inherit your grandmother's wedding ring, your grandfather's War medals, a lock of your mother's hair or your father's stamp collection. Write about a family heirloom that you have already been given, one that you have been told you will receive or one that you would like to inherit when you get older.

heirloom: any bit of personal property handed down in a family for generations

Example: A Picture's Worth a Thousand Words

My great grandparents had a professional photographer take portraits of their families. These old, curled and yellowed pictures are still in my family, generations later. Some are in picture frames. Others are in an old shoe box that my mother keeps on the top shelf of her bedroom cupboard. These sepia photographs passed first to my grandparents and then to my mother and father. Someday, they will pass to me, and then I will hand them down to my children. These pictures are all that remain of my ancestors who lived long ago. They are worth more than a thousand words—and much more than a thousand dollars. They are priceless and fragile family heirlooms.

Activity 50

You've Got Your Mother's Eyes

When we hear the word **inheritance**, often images of wealth and property pop into our heads. But we inherit much more from our ancestors than money and material possessions—and not all of it is good! Think about one good physical characteristic and one positive personality trait that you have inherited from your parents or grandparents. Now put the shoe on the other foot and think of two "not so good" examples.

Example: My Inheritance
- I inherited from my mother her lovely, thick hair. (good, physical characteristic)
- I inherited from my father his easy, friendly nature. (good, personality trait)
- I inherited from my mother her migraine headaches. (bad, physical characteristic)
- I inherited from my father his impulsive spending habits. (bad, personality trait)

Activity 51

The Luck of the Irish

Rightly or wrongly, we often attribute certain personality traits to their countries of origin and behavioral/physical characteristics to specific races. The Nordic races tend to be blond-haired and blue-eyed, for example, while the Slavic races generally exhibit dark hair and eyes. French people are renowned for their "joie de vivre" (joy of life), while Italians are said to be passionate. These fixed generalizations are called "stereotypes." While there may be some foundation to them, these stereotypes are not absolute cultural truths. Talk to your parents about your ancestry. Where did your mother's mother come from? What about your father's father? What "national attributes" show up in your personality?

Example: Celtic Determination
My ancestors were British, Scottish, Irish, French, German and Pennsylvania Dutch. Among other traits, I have certainly inherited the stubbornness of a Scot. The luck of the Irish, unfortunately, skipped my generation!

Activity 52

Heritage Days

One way in which we pass our traditions to future generations is through the celebration of our heritage. Martin Luther King Jr. Day, Presidents' Day, International Women's Day, St. Patrick's Day, Victoria Day (Canada), Memorial Day, Flag Day, Canada Day (Canada), Veterans Day, Remembrance Day (Canada) and Thanksgiving Day are holidays that help us celebrate our past and commemorate the achievements and sacrifices of our ancestors. Choose one of these special holidays and describe how its celebration helps you to understand and appreciate your heritage and your cultural identity.

Example: Remembrance Day

In Canada, November 11th is a day set aside for remembering and honoring those who fought and died for the freedom of our country. On Remembrance Day we think about how fortunate we are to live in a fair and democratic nation. We think about how freedom has defined who and what we are as Canadians. We think about how lucky we are to have so much and want for so little. We think about peace and what it means to live without fear and despair. We give thanks for all of the brave men and women who sacrificed their lives so that we could continue to enjoy ours. And we think about what our country and our people might be like had those soldiers and civilians not made their ultimate sacrifice. On Remembrance Day we think about the high price of freedom. We think about the thousands of people who paid for that freedom with the last beat of their hearts. We give thanks for their monumental gift and acknowledge that our Canadian heritage is worth defending with our lives: that we, too, would sacrifice our lives in the name of generations of Canadians to come.

Activity 53

Flying High

Think about your country's flag.
What does the symbolic design on the flag mean to you?
To your country? What relevance did these symbols have to the people who first settled in or helped to shape your country?
How do you feel when you see your flag flying high?

flag: a piece of light cloth, usually bunting or silk, bearing some symbolic design and chiefly used as an emblem or standard indicating nationality

Example: The Flag of Ornika (planet of our little alien friend, Znorb from Activity 47)

To Znorb, his or her or its flag symbolizes the triumph of Ornikian life. Because the "people" of Ornik had to flee their dying solar system and colonize another planet in a far-away galaxy, Znorb thinks of his or her or its flag as a victory banner that celebrates the Ornikians' successful battle against extinction. The black color represents the unending cavern of space; the burst of light is simultaneously evocative of the gaseous expulsions from the rocket boosters of the spaceship that transported the Ornikian survivors to their new home and the explosive death of the Ornikian sun; the star is the sun at the center of the Ornikians' new solar system, Ornikinaga; the Ornikian footprint symbolizes colonization of a barren and previously uninhabited planet; the water droplet inside the rock indicates the Ornikians' ability to penetrate the planet's rocky shelf and access the life-sustaining water trapped below and the Gripnot reflects the Ornikians' conquest over the inhospitable climate of their new planet, Ornika, through the production of food. The flag is circular to represent at once the fullness of life and the biodome that is the Ornikians' answer to shelter, protection and propagation in their brave new world. Since Znorb is only a second-generation Ornikagian, and therefore a pioneer, everyone on his or her or its planet has the same appreciation for the symbols on their flag. When Znorb sees the flag of Ornika flying high inside the biodome he or she or it feels a swelling of pride, thankfulness and hope inside his or her or its little green heart.

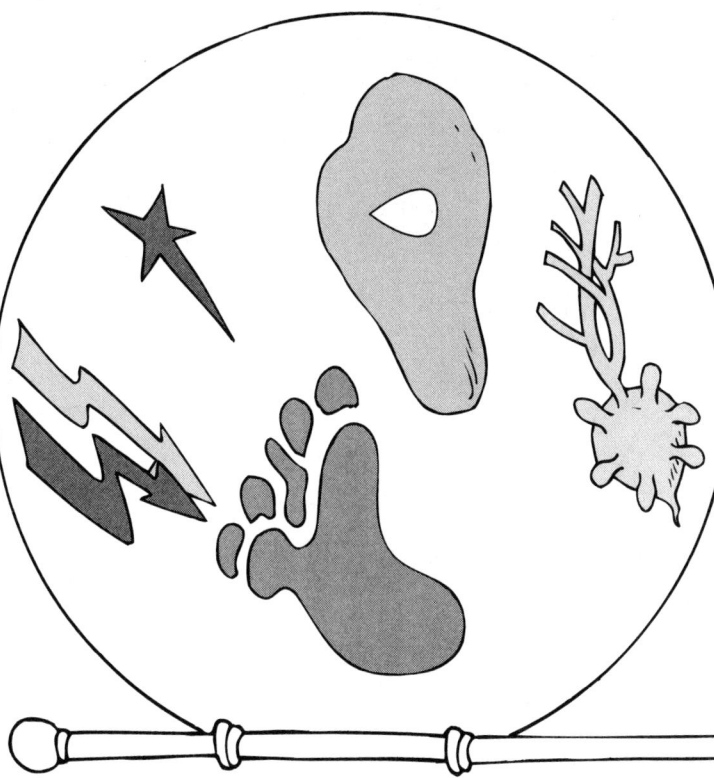

Activity 54

Aesthetics/Athletics

You can also celebrate your heritage through art and recreation. Think of the kind of music, dance, crafts and sports that you like and about your interests and special talents. How can you relate your participation in and enjoyment of these activities to your parents or grandparents?

Examples:
- I play the piano. My great uncle was one of Canada's finest concert pianists.
- I played the clarinet. My great-grandfather was a clarinetist.
- My father loves car racing. I met my husband (an ex-race car driver) at a racetrack.
- I paint with watercolor. My mom paints with watercolor. I love to write. My aunt is a prolific letter writer.
- I love to read. My mom loves to read.
- I am an editor. My mom is a proofreader. My dad was a printer.
- I love nature and animals. So do both my parents.
- I love my parents so much that I am a parent today.

When it comes right down to it (although I would like to think that I am very much my own person), I am definitely a sum of all that my parents and grandparents are and were before me. I can relate just about everything I do and love to my relatives, particularly to my parents.

Activity 55

Food for Thought

The foods you eat, especially at celebrations and on festive holidays, can give clues to your cultural heritage. Design a menu that is filled with traditional family food items and think of a name for your menu or the restaurant that might serve such fare. See if a friend can identify your cultural background from your menu.

Example: Coveart's Catch of the Day

Appetizer
  deep-fried jumbo shrimp

Entree
  fresh bread
  jellied salad
  beer-battered halibut
  fresh-cut fries
  crispy onion rings

Dessert
  apple crisp
  fruit cobbler
  lemon meringue pie

Beverages
  milk
  soda
  tea
  coffee

From this menu, I think people might be able to guess at the British and Pennsylvania Dutch heritage in my cultural heritage.

Activity 56

Cultural Comparisons

Communities can be made up of many cultures. Think about the other kids in your class. Do you share the same cultural background? Choose a partner and compare and contrast your personalities, life-styles and cultural heritage. What are the similarities? What are the differences? (You might want to examine physical characteristics and traditions such as food, clothing, celebrations, art and recreation, special holidays, religious beliefs, names . . . .)

Example: Jonathan and Tracey

Jonathan's parents hail from Britain. Mine were born and raised in Canada. My husband and I are as alike as we are different. Many of these similarities and differences can be traced to our parents and our cultural upbringing. (I'll mark these with an asterisk*!)

Jonathan
*likes cars
*works full-time
*drives sports car
*standoffish
*reads magazines
loves computers
tolerates pets
vast general knowledge

*conservative dresser
not fond of sweets
likes to discard things

*blue eyes
*balding
*skinny
*no middle name
*tall
loves country life
avoids confrontation

*university graduate

Tracey
*likes animals
*works part-time
drives mini van
*touchy/feely
*reads books
*tolerates computers
*loves pets
*very little memory of anything beyond yesterday
flamboyant dresser
*loves sweet things
*develops strong attachments
*brown eyes
*graying
*stocky
*middle name
*tall
*loves country life
avoids confrontation at all costs
university graduate

Activity 58

Cultural Celebrations Community Style

Think of an annual celebration that is held in your community. How does this celebration reflect your heritage and cultural identity?

Example: Steamboats on Scugog

The Lake Scugog Historical Society strives to preserve our local heritage. This year it is organizing the first annual Steamboats on Scugog Festival to commemorate the important role that these watercraft and their operators played in the historical development of the Port Perry community. The Woodman was the first steamboat built at the waterfront. It and dozens of others traversed the shores of Lake Scugog supplying lumber mills and carrying people and produce to local ports. These steamboats and their cargo laid the economic foundation for Port Perry and other communities in the Lake Scugog basin. The Steamboats on Scugog celebration is intended to stimulate civic interest in a by-gone era and appreciation for the people whose contributions made this time—and this town—so historically significant.

Activity 57

Delicious Diversity

Survey the kids in your class to find out their cultural backgrounds. Tabulate the number of times each culture is represented in your classroom. Put this information on a chart with **Number of Students** on the vertical axis and **Cultural Origin** on the horizontal axis. (If possible, compare your chart to that of another classroom. Are the two charts similar or very different? In what way?

Example: When you're done, you might have a chart that looks like this . . .

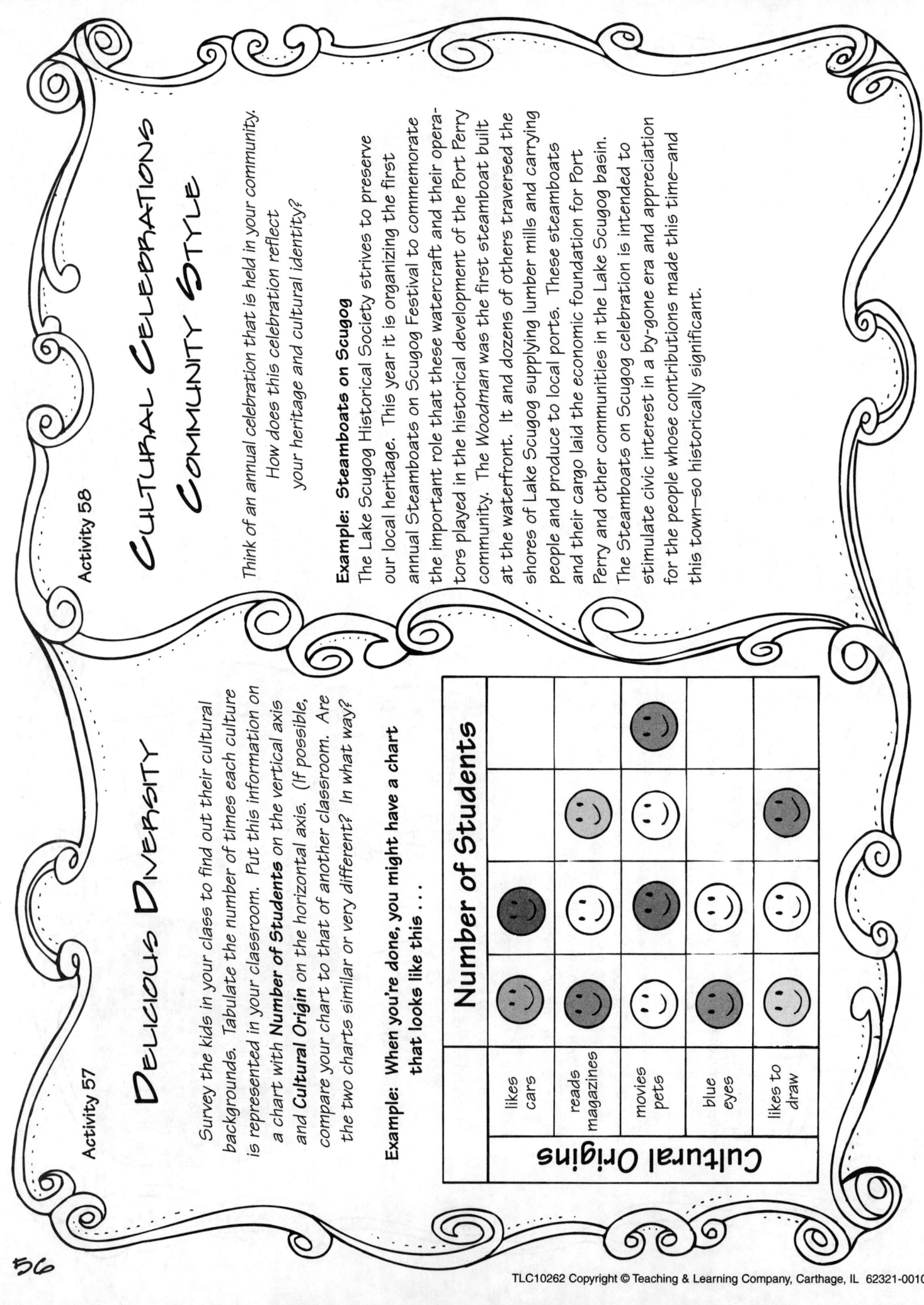

Activity 59

COMMUNITY CONTRIBUTIONS

We all contribute to the growth and well-being of our communities: by voting in elections, paying our taxes, providing services, through our work . . .

1. What do you and the other members of your family do to make your community a better place?
2. What special contributions have people of different cultures made to your community? (Think about restaurants, special services, the arts, retail stores, etc.)

Example 1: Our Contributions

I help out at my kids' schools, offering creative writing workshops, assisting in the classroom, working at special events and supervising field trips. I have also served as a board member for a number of different community organizations.

As a family we have improved our property enormously since taking ownership. This has in turn improved the appearance of our neighborhood. We never litter and often pick up trash left by other people. We help to preserve the natural environment by rescuing animals in distress and replanting trees in deforested places on our six acres. We carpool to reduce pollution. We help to raise money for charity and canvas door-to-door during fundraising drives. On occasion, we circulate petitions and attend meetings on social issues of concern to the members of our community and society at large.

Example 2: The Contributions of Others

Other cultures contribute much to our community. A Dutch family operates Emiels, a restaurant featuring cultural cuisine. An East Indian family operates a gas station and convenience store. A Polish sculptor offers classes in soapstone carving.

Days Gone By

In this section, students draw on their knowledge of the days of early settlement to compare and contrast present-day life with life in pioneer times. They develop an appreciation for the contributions of early settlers and an understanding of how dramatically life has changed in the last few hundred years. They examine the impact of industrialization, technology and modern sophistication on everyday existence and discuss the relative pros and cons of life in both periods. Specifically, they . . .

- compare and contrast the lives of pioneer and present-day children of similar ages (Activity 60)
- compare and contrast life in a pioneer settlement with that in their own community (Activity 61)
- compare and contrast buildings in a pioneer settlement with those of the present day (Activity 62)
- compare tools used by the pioneers to today's tools (Activity 63)
- identify the improvements to medicine and health care (Activity 64)
- compare past and present means of communication (Activity 65)
- compare past and present forms of recreation (Activity 66)
- compare pioneer diet and foods to that of present-day people (Activity 67)
- identify significant heritage symbols on their country's coat of arms (Activity 68)
- create a coat of arms for their own family, school or community (Activity 69)
- consider the pros and cons of life today and in days gone by (Activity 70)

Note: Because these exercises are more objective than subjective and are based as much on observation as personal experience, and because the author does not wish to lead or limit the creative thought and expression of the writers, she has declined to include examples for much of this section.

Activity 61

Easier or Harder?

How was life in a pioneer settlement different than it is today in your own community? (Think of services, jobs, schools, stores, use of natural resources . . . .)

Activity 60

More Fun, Less Work?

Using your knowledge of the early settlement or colonization of your community or country, compare your life and daily routine to the life of a pioneer child of your age.

Is your life simpler or more complicated?
Is your workload heavier or lighter than that of your pioneer compatriot?
Do you have more fun or less?
Does life today offer more possibilities or fewer?

Activity 63

Cool Tools

What kinds of tools did pioneers use to do their work?
What kinds of tools do we use today to do the same work?
Think of an occupation today that existed in pioneer times (carpenter, doctor, teacher, restaurateur, hotelier . . .). Use this as your title. Divide your page into two columns, headed **Then** and **Now**. List the implements used by people in both time periods to do the same job.

Activity 62

From Post and Beam to Bricks and Mortar

Compare your house, school, hospital, convenience or grocery store, fire station, local hotel or motel, restaurant, etc., to the same buildings that might have existed in a pioneer settlement.
Choose at least one and draw pictures to illustrate both the long ago and present-day versions of these structures.

Activity 65

Talk and Travel

How did people in pioneer communities communicate? How did they travel? How do we communicate and travel today? What methods are common to both groups? What methods are different?

*Using three columns, headed **Then, Then and Now** and **Now**, list the methods of talk and travel that have been used over the last several hundred years. What are your all-time favorite modes of communication and transportation? Why?*

Activity 64

Here's to Your Health

Think about how medicine and health care have changed since pioneer times.

What do present-day doctors carry in their medical bags that pioneer doctors did not?

What happens to you when you get sick, and why are your chances of recovery better than those of a pioneer child?

Activity 67

The Evolution of Food

Compare the pioneer diet to your own.
How have snacks, beverages, three square meals a day (breakfast, lunch and dinner) and restaurant foods changed?
How much does this change have to do with modern methods of food production and storage and technology?

Activity 66

Fun and Frolic

What did pioneers do for fun?
Compare your methods of rest, relaxation and recreation to those of children and adults in days gone by.
Ask a parent and an older adult (a grandparent, perhaps?) what he or she used to do in his or her leisure time. What toys were popular?
What sports? What games?
Is it more fun to play today than it was yesterday?

TLC10262 Copyright © Teaching & Learning Company, Carthage, IL 62321-0010

Activity 69

Create a Coat/Bill/Coin/Stamp

Develop a culturally symbolic coat of arms, bill, coin or stamp for your family, school, community or country. Explain the significance of your design and the reasons behind your choice of symbols.

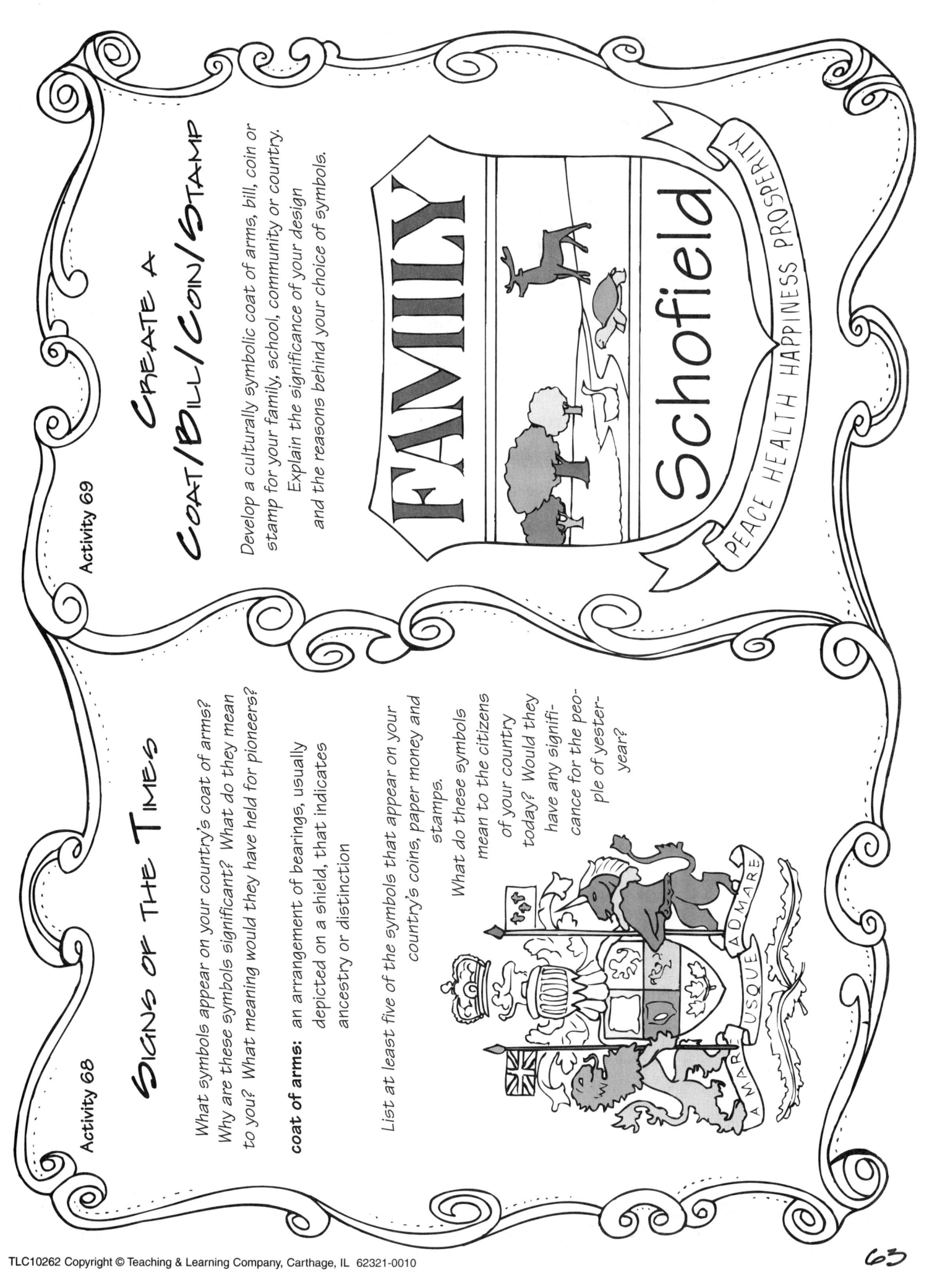

Activity 68

Signs of the Times

What symbols appear on your country's coat of arms? Why are these symbols significant? What do they mean to you? What meaning would they have held for pioneers?

coat of arms: an arrangement of bearings, usually depicted on a shield, that indicates ancestry or distinction

List at least five of the symbols that appear on your country's coins, paper money and stamps.

What do these symbols mean to the citizens of your country today? Would they have any significance for the people of yesteryear?

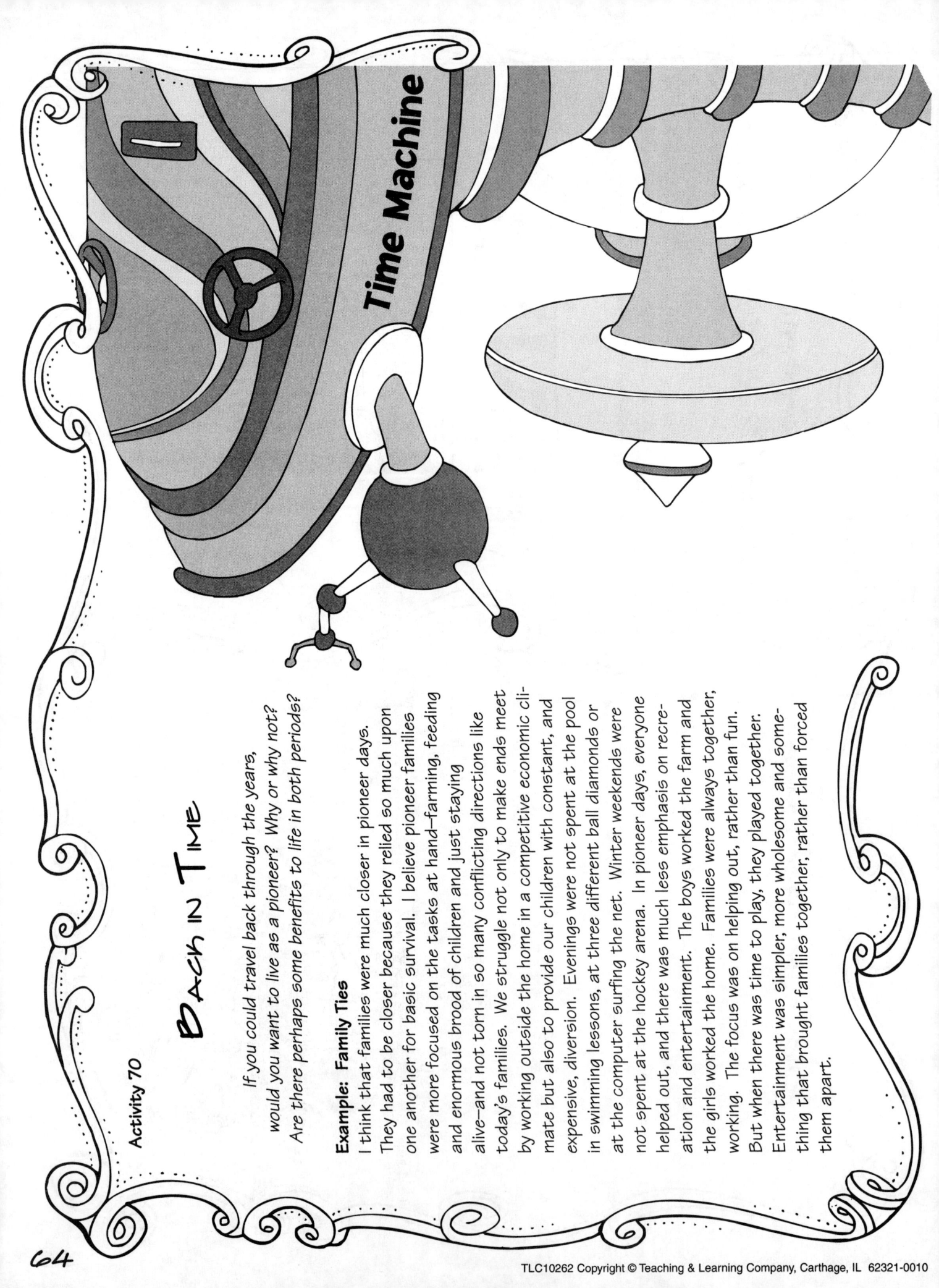

Activity 70

Back in Time

If you could travel back through the years, would you want to live as a pioneer? Why or why not? Are there perhaps some benefits to life in both periods?

Example: Family Ties

I think that families were much closer in pioneer days. They had to be closer because they relied so much upon one another for basic survival. I believe pioneer families were more focused on the tasks at hand—farming, feeding and enormous brood of children and just staying alive—and not torn in so many conflicting directions like today's families. We struggle not only to make ends meet by working outside the home in a competitive economic climate but also to provide our children with constant, and expensive, diversion. Evenings were not spent at the pool in swimming lessons, at three different ball diamonds or at the computer surfing the net. Winter weekends were not spent at the hockey arena. In pioneer days, everyone helped out, and there was much less emphasis on recreation and entertainment. The boys worked the farm and the girls worked the home. Families were always together, working. The focus was on helping out, rather than fun. But when there was time to play, they played together. Entertainment was simpler, more wholesome and something that brought families together, rather than forced them apart.

My Community

In this section, students investigate family needs and how people in their community live, work, travel and interact. They identify important buildings and places in their communities, and use directional language, symbols and recognizable landmarks to map important routes and destinations within the community. They record significant information about themselves and their school and describe their home and community in familiar terms. Specifically, they . . .

- demonstrate an understanding of basic personal and family needs and identify how these needs are met (Activity 71)
- identify buildings in their community and the uses of these buildings (Activity 72)
- identify the occupations of people in the community; identify the buildings in which they work; describe the tools and vehicles they use to do their jobs; show how these people play an important role in meeting the needs of families (Activity 73)
- identify safe places in the community (Activity 74)
- identify ways in which people travel around the community (Activity 75)
- develop an understanding of infrastructure and "hidden" infrastructure (Activity 76)
- identify significant events, places and celebrations (Activity 77)
- describe how families and friends in the community interact (Activity 78)
- examine the importance of volunteerism to healthy communities (Activity 79)
- recall and record specific information about their community, their school and themselves (Activity 80)
- identify and describe routes within the school and home using familiar symbols and landmarks (Activity 81)
- describe the route to school, using familiar landmarks and symbols (Activity 82)
- draw a map and use symbols to identify buildings and places in their community (Activity 83)
- draw a simple grid map and locate familiar places using number and letter coordinates (Activity 84)
- describe their home and community in familiar terms (Activity 85)

Activity 71

Needy Beings

Human beings all over the world have four basic needs: food, water, shelter and protection.
If these needs are not met, we cannot survive.
Explain how you and your family are able to meet each one of these needs.
Describe what might happen if you were suddenly deprived of one of these basic necessities.

Example: The Naked Truth

One way that I am able to protect my children is by providing them with clothes. If I were suddenly unable to offer them a winter coat, mittens and a hat, they would not be able to survive even brief periods of exposure to the harsh winter elements. With local temperatures dropping as low as -52° with the windchill, their skin would freeze before they walked the four minutes to the bus. Without clothes (and sunscreen!) in the summer, I would not be able to protect them from the blistering heat of the sun's ultraviolet rays. Without clothes they would be eaten alive by mosquitoes and flies in the spring. Without shoes and boots, I couldn't protect their feet from the winter ice and snow, the heat of asphalt in the summer or the boggy dampness of the spring and fall. Without clothes I could not protect their knees and elbows from cuts and scrapes when they fall. And, of course, without clothes I could not prevent them from being "indecently exposed" whenever they left the privacy of our home!

Activity 72

Super Structures

Think of 10 different kinds of buildings that are found in your community. What is the purpose of each of these buildings? Directly or indirectly, how do you and your family members use these 10 buildings?
(Use headings and columns to organize your thoughts.)

Example:
Building
silo

Purpose
to store grain before transportation to a refining facility

Family Use
My family purchases and consumes grain products (such as flour and bread) that might have been stored in this silo (indirect use).

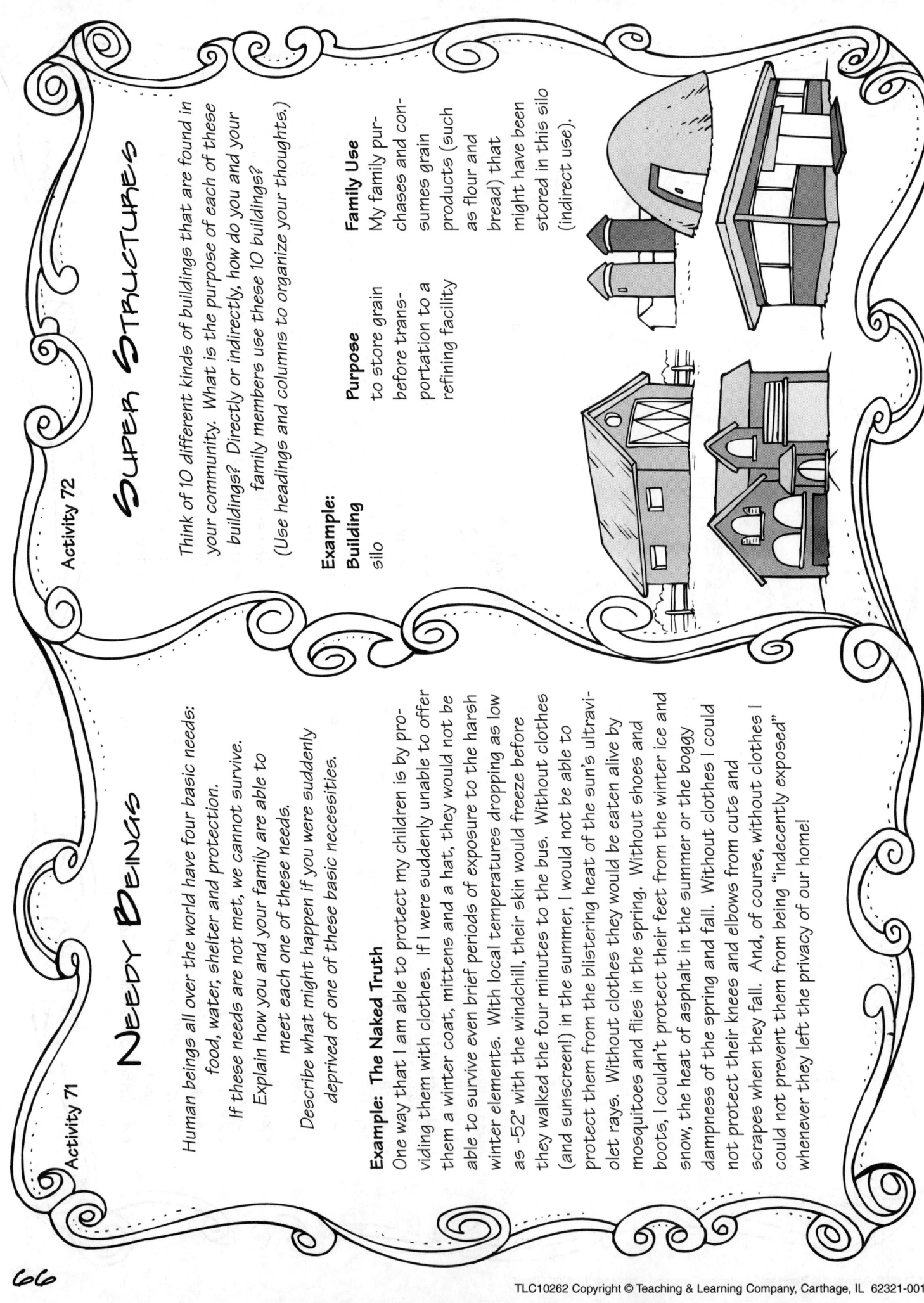

Activity 73

People at Work

Healthy communities are diverse communities. It is the different kinds of work that people do every day that allow the places in which we live to thrive.

1. List the occupations of 10 different people in your community. (No two people on your list should do the same job.)

   Use four columns to:
   - List the occupation of each of your 10 people.
   - Identify the buildings in which each person works.
   - Describe the tools and vehicles they use to do their jobs.
   - Explain how each of these people contributes to the well-being of your family and your community. (In other words, how do they help to meet your needs for food, water, shelter and protection?)

2. Draw a picture of one of your 10 people at his or her place of work. Label the picture to include the information you have recorded in your columns.

Example:

Occupation	Place of Work	Tools/Vehicles	Contributions
Secretary	School (in the office)	• computer • telephone • P.A. system • filing cabinets • first aid kit	• handles requests/complaints • deals with correspondence • makes announcements • fills out late slips • deals with sick/injured kids • greets visitors • manages principal's schedule • keeps school running smooth

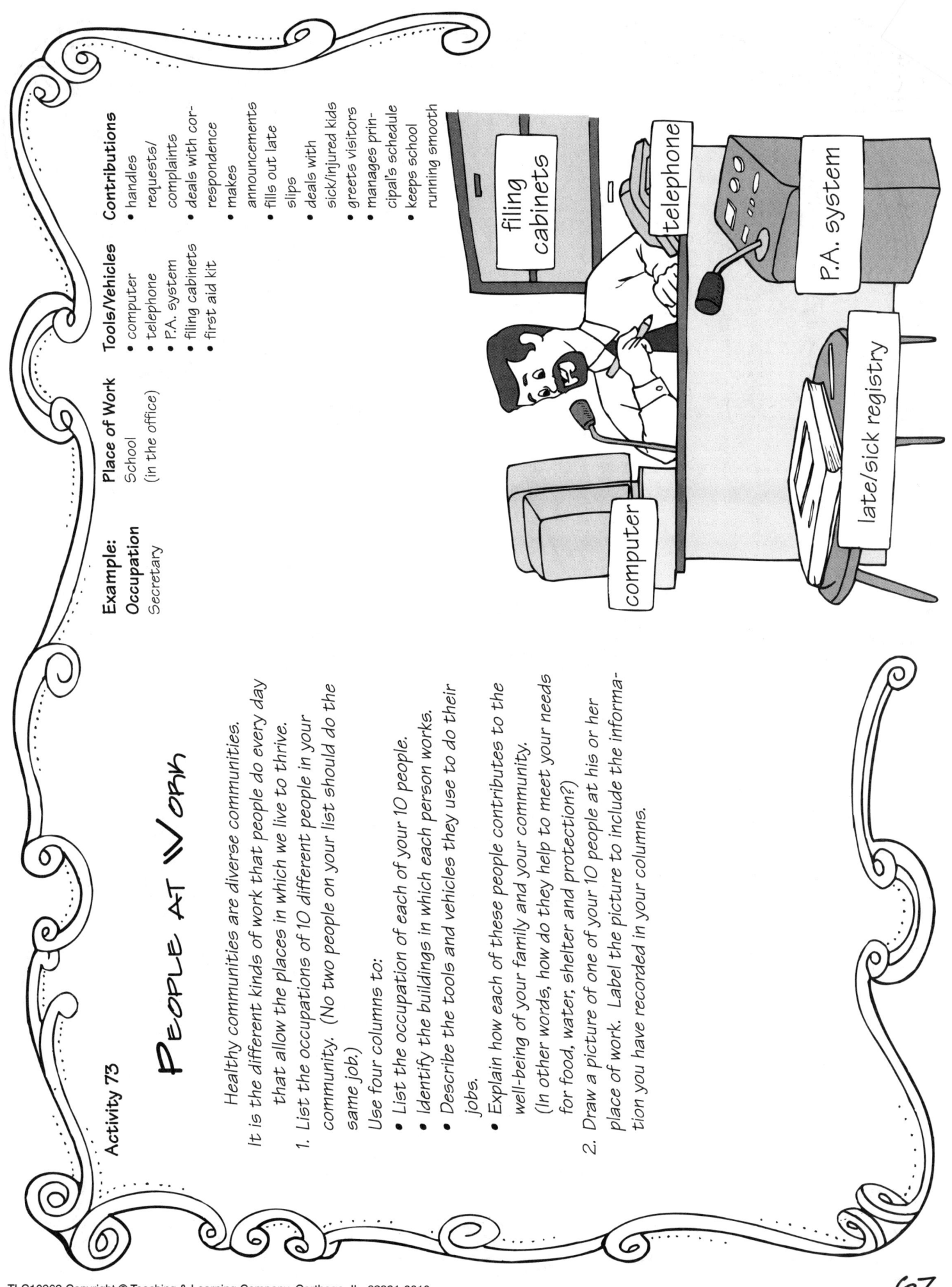

Activity 74

Safe and Sound

List five "safe" places in your community. How do these places and the people in them keep you safe?

Example: A Block Parent's House
A house with a "block parent" sign in the window is a safe haven for children who are in any kind of trouble or danger. Block parents have been carefully screened and are considered trustworthy. They know what to do and whom to contact in case of an emergency. Block parents are "safe" strangers.

Activity 75

Getting Around

Name at least five ways in which people travel around your community.

Of the five:
- Which is the quickest way to travel?
- Which is the most pleasurable?
- Which is the least expensive?
- Which mode of transportation gives you the greatest degree of flexibility?
- Which is the best for the environment?

(You're on your own for this one. But remember: transportation is "the state of being carried from one place to another." As long as it gets you from here to there, it is a mode of transportation. Try to include at least two unconventional modes of conveyance on your list.)

TLC10262 Copyright © Teaching & Learning Company, Carthage, IL 62321-0010

Activity 76

Secret Systems

Infrastructure is described as "the permanent foundation or essential elements of a structure, system, plan of operations, etc.: especially, the essential installations of a community, as schools, hospitals, transportation facilities, power plants, etc."

Think about the "hidden" infrastructure in your community: sewers, water mains, hydro lines, telephone wires, etc. Where does the "stuff" go when you flush the toilet? What makes it possible for clean drinking water to pour from the spout when you turn on the tap? How are you able to call your best friend on the telephone? Why does the light go on when you flip the switch?

Use your imagination to draw a diagram of one of these hidden systems, from its source—or starting point—all the way to your house. Label the important parts of the system to show how it works. (Don't limit yourself to what is real or possible. Be creative. Be inventive. Most of all, be descriptive!)

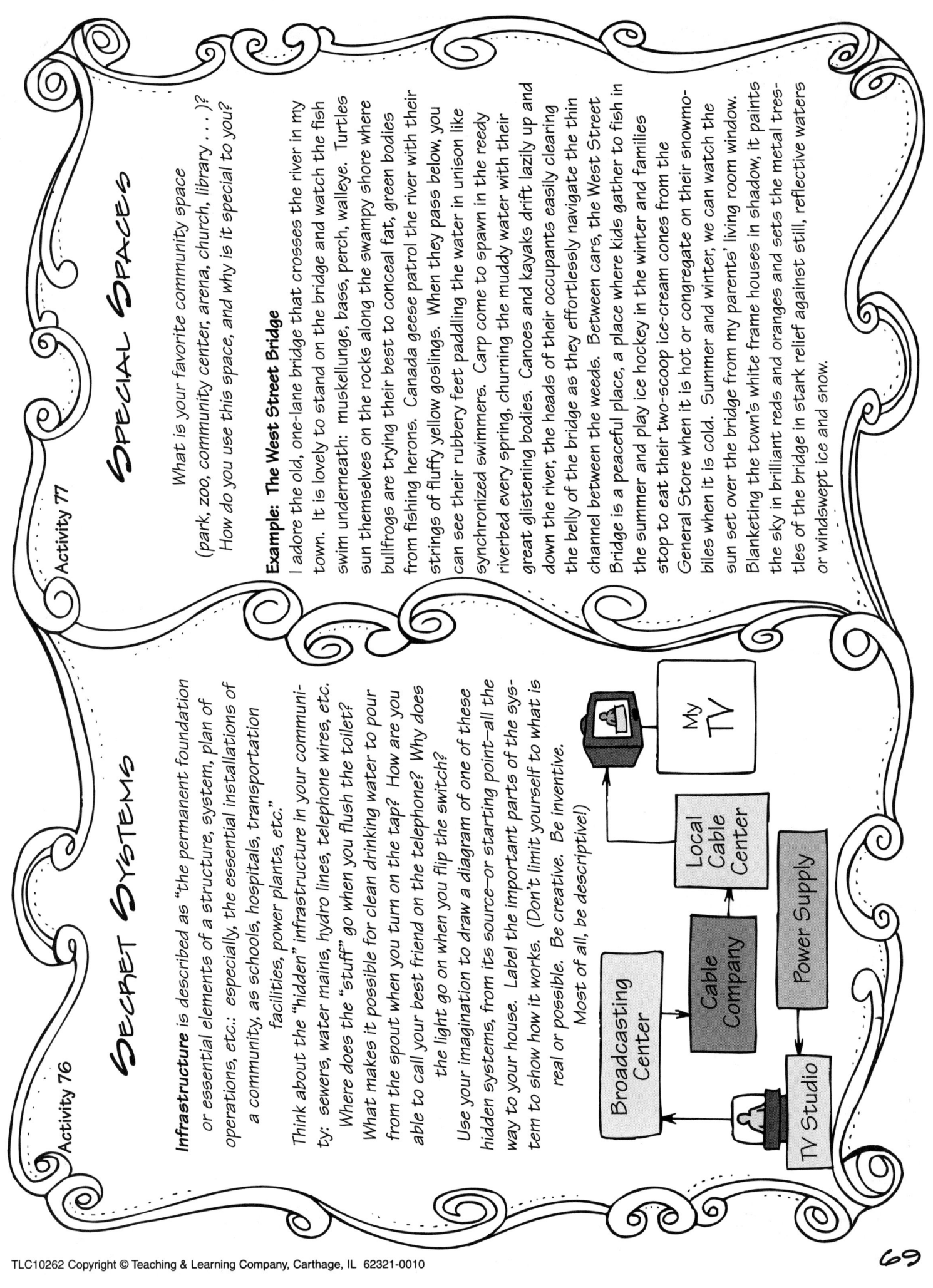

Activity 77

Special Spaces

What is your favorite community space (park, zoo, community center, arena, church, library . . .)? How do you use this space, and why is it special to you?

Example: The West Street Bridge

I adore the old, one-lane bridge that crosses the river in my town. It is lovely to stand on the bridge and watch the fish swim underneath: muskellunge, bass, perch, walleye. Turtles sun themselves on the rocks along the swampy shore where bullfrogs are trying their best to conceal fat, green bodies from fishing herons. Canada geese patrol the river with their strings of fluffy yellow goslings. When they pass below, you can see their rubbery feet paddling the water in unison like synchronized swimmers. Carp come to spawn in the reedy riverbed every spring, churning the muddy water with their great glistening bodies. Canoes and kayaks drift lazily up and down the river, the heads of their occupants easily clearing the belly of the bridge as they effortlessly navigate the thin channel between the weeds. Between cars, the West Street Bridge is a peaceful place, a place where kids gather to fish in the summer and play ice hockey in the winter and families stop to eat their two-scoop ice-cream cones from the General Store when it is hot or congregate on their snowmobiles when it is cold. Summer and winter, we can watch the sun set over the bridge from my parents' living room window. Blanketing the town's white frame houses in shadow, it paints the sky in brilliant reds and oranges and sets the metal trestles of the bridge in stark relief against still, reflective waters or windswept ice and snow.

Activity 78

Community Central

How do you and your family members interact with other people in your community? Describe one community event that brings people together.

Example: Winter on the River

Many things bring the people of my community together: church dinners, pig roasts, movie nights, curling bonspiels and mail collection at the general store. Every January one of our North Road neighbor families hosts a Winter on the River post-Christmas get-together. They clear the ice for skating and hockey, light a fire at the edge of the river and take the kids for "crack the whip" rides on snowracers that are tethered in a line behind an aging snowmobile. When dusk obscures the river, the chilly revelers move indoors to enjoy a sumptuous potluck dinner. Kids wolf down their food and then chase around the house while the adults balance laden paper plates on their laps and try to make conversation above the happy racket. Hours later, people drift away on snowmobiles or on foot pulling toboggans loaded with sleeping children and leftovers. This annual gathering is a wonderful way for the members of the North Road community to maintain contact through the cold months and to make the most of a Canadian winter on the river.

Activity 79

Volunteers Are VIPs

Volunteers are VIPs—Very Important People—and they play a key role in keeping our communities healthy. Volunteers do not expect any type of payment or reward for their services on behalf of others, and many people rely heavily on their good deeds and charitable works. Volunteers coach recreational sports teams, organize and help at special events, teach Sunday school, raise money for community projects and local charities, visit with and deliver food to the sick and the elderly, provide fire-fighting services . . . . Has an adult that you know ever volunteered to do anything special for someone else? Have you ever volunteered to do something for somebody without expecting or accepting a reward—chores for your mom or dad, perhaps, without the promise of an allowance or yard work for a neighbor without taking payment?

Example 1: Granny Helen

One of our caregivers, Granny Helen, has for years volunteered her time and her vehicle to deliver meals to the frail, the elderly, the sick and the isolated in her community. For this work she expects nothing in return save for the good feeling it gives her to do something nice for someone else.

Example 2: Involuntary Volunteerism

Often we act as volunteers without even realizing it! The other day, I "volunteered" to drive an elderly lady across town so that she would not have to walk in the rain. The same day, Matthew "volunteered" in the school library at recess (helping to shelve books in preparation for summer vacation) and Patrick "volunteered" to help his struggling baseball coach carry the equipment bag to his car.

70

Activity 81
Finding My Way

Using directional language (north, south, east, west) and familiar landmarks (the drinking fountain, the girls' washroom . . .) and symbols (exit sign, room number plate . . .) describe how to get to another room or place in the school—the office, the front door, the library, the gymnasium, etc.—from your classroom.

Describe how to get to the nearest exit.

In the case of a fire, has your teacher mapped out a fire route that you are to follow? If so, describe it.

Example: Kitchen to Office

(Since I no longer attend school, I am going to describe how to travel from one room to another in my house.)

To get to my basement office from my main floor kitchen . . . I must travel west along the carpeted hallway, past the laundry room on the right (north) side of the house and past the powder room (also on the right) until I reach a large, front foyer tiled in ceramic. When I reach the foyer, I turn right (north) to face the double front doors. I walk towards the doors and then turn left when I am two feet from the door handle. I walk several steps until I come to a carpeted threshold and a painted wrought iron railing. Then I walk down three stairs (heading west), make a 45° turn to the left on the landing and walk down 10 more stairs to another landing. Turn to the right (45° again), and I descend two more stairs. I am now in the basement. From here I walk forward (west) until I reach a demiwall that separates the kitchen in our basement apartment from the living room. I turn to my right again (45°) and head north until I come to another wall. Doors open off this small hallway to my left and right. I turn right 45° (I am now facing east) and walk through the door. There! I have successfully navigated a trip to my basement office.

Activity 80
My Community, My School and Me

Complete this personal survey and record some simple facts and feelings about your community, your school and yourself.

- I was born in: _____ (country plus city, town, village)
- at: _____ (name of hospital or other place of birth)
- on: _____ (month/day/year)
- I have _____ (color) hair, _____ (color) eyes and a great _____ (physical or character feature)
- In my family there are: _____ (list family members)
- My current address is: _____
- My phone number is: _____
- I attend: _____ (name of school)
- I am in grade: _____ (state grade level)
- My teacher's name is: _____
- The best thing about my school is: _____
- The name of my community is: _____
- The approximate population of my community is: _____
- My community is special because: _____
- I help my community by: _____

Activity 82

Follow Me

Describe the route you take to get to school each day. Use directional language and landmarks. Draw a map of your route using pictures and symbols.

Example: From 12 North Road to 87 West Street

(I am going to describe how I get to my parents' house every day . . . yes, every day!)

1. Walk to the end of the driveway.
2. Turn left.
3. Walk along the gravel road to the stop sign on the right.
4. Turn left and walk around the telephone pole.
5. Walk along the split rail cedar fence.
6. Follow the curve in the road. (It bears right.)
7. Start to jog at the piles of dirt beside the red brick bungalow on the left.
8. Jog past the barn and the three cows in the field on the south side of the road.
9. At the T-junction (Highway 2 and North Road), turn left.
10. Jog on the grass between the big maple tree and the "no exit" sign.
11. Jog up a slight incline to the paved side road that runs south, parallel to the highway.
12. Jog down this sloped street (passing a pond and waterfall, a family of black wooden bears and a small herd of wooden deer) to the T-junction at the bottom.
13. Turn right and jog west to the stop sign at the junction of Bruce and Highway 2.
14. Between cars, sprint diagonally across the highway to West Street.
15. Walk quickly uphill (north) following the right-hand curve in the road (past the Northwind Ranch sign on the left) to the crest of the hill.
16. At the fenced donkey paddock on the left, jog and delight in the scenic beauty of the farms spreading down and away to the west.
17. At the bottom of the hill, just before the West Street Bridge, turn right (east) at the black lamppost with the 87 sign.
18. Jog up the slightly winding paved driveway, past the tamarack tree on the left, to the parking area at the top. (There is a log house on the left and a garage on the right.)
19. Bank left. (Wave to father, tinkering with something mechanical in the garage, on the way past.)
20. Take two steps further to the north and collapse in a sweaty heap, calling loudly for mother to bring a stretcher.

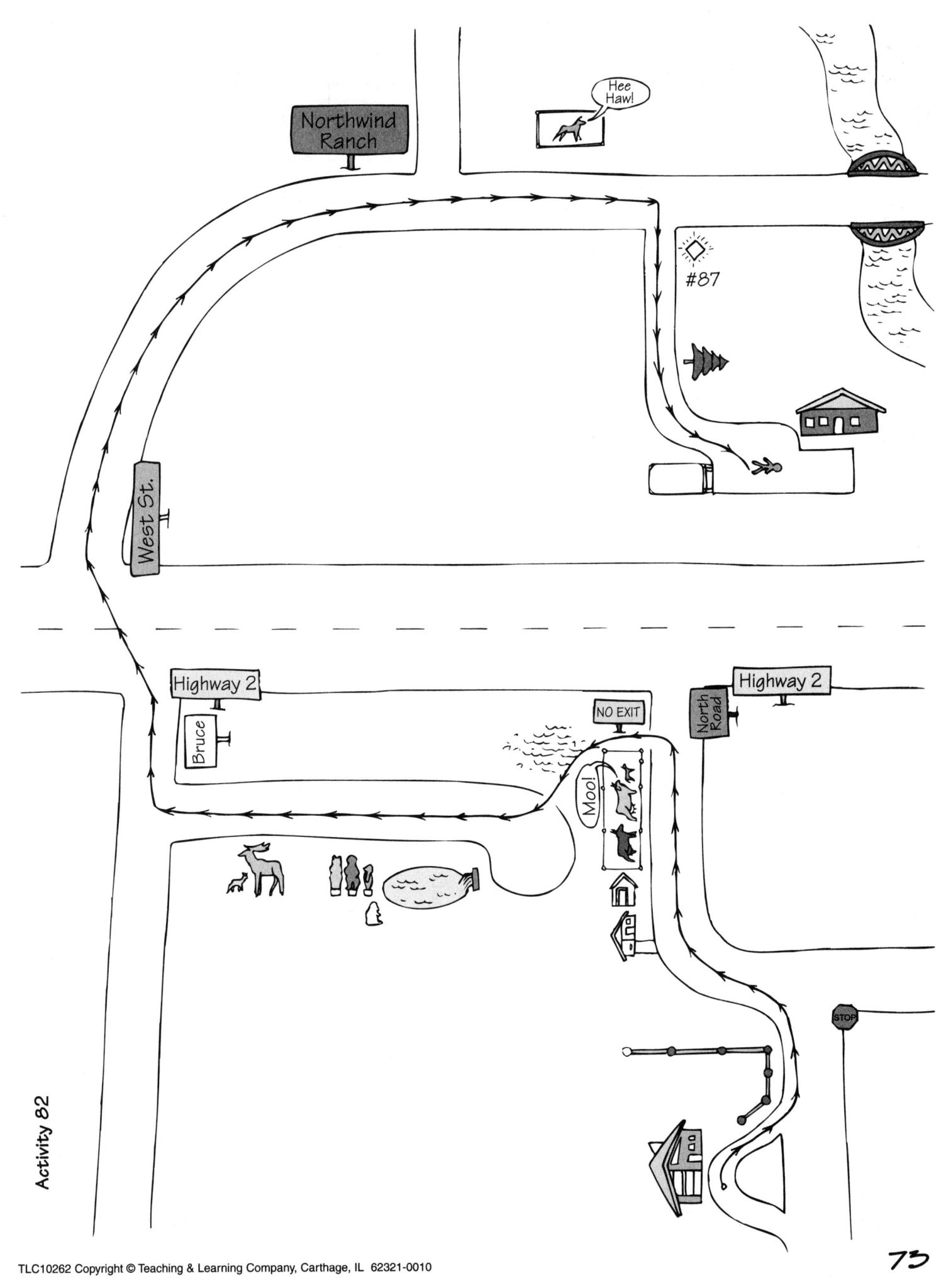

Activity 83

Junior Cartographers
(Mini Mapmakers)

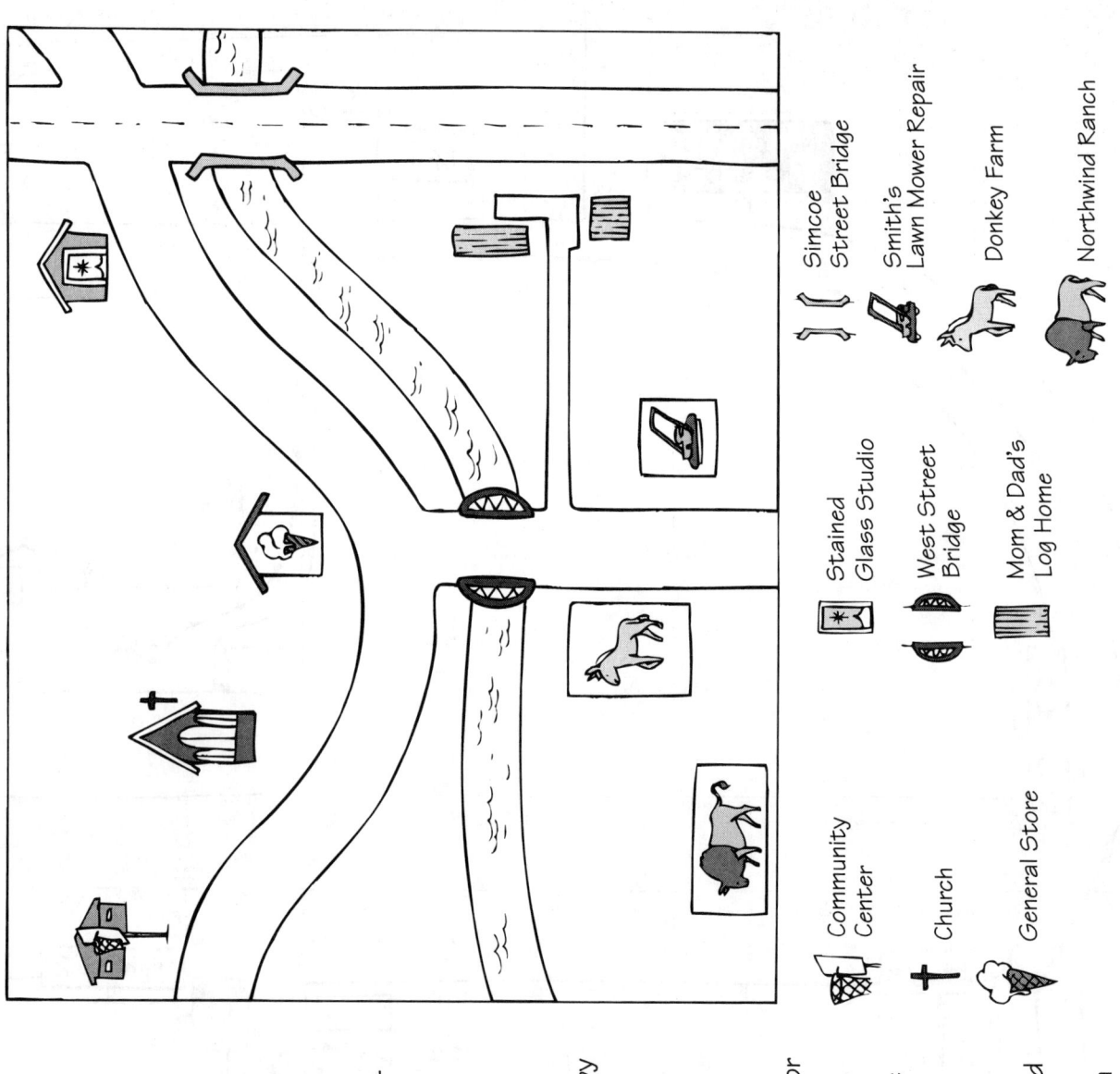

1. Draw a simple map of your community using signs and symbols to identify buildings and local landmarks. Make a legend for your symbols so that anyone reading your map will know what they represent.

2. Describe one of the "famous" landmarks in your community. What does this landmark signify to you? To others? If you can, write a brief history of this landmark (when/why it was erected or named, by whom, etc.)

landmark: any familiar, conspicuous or memorable object, especially one on land, used as a guide either by travellers on land or by navigators

Example 2: The Shoe Tree

I don't know who first started the shoe tree, or when the first pair of shoes was nailed to that old trunk, but it is a marker for all who are travelling south on Simcoe Street (or at least to kids who are tired of driving) that they are about to enter the town of Whitby. The shoe tree is in an old swamp. A very tall stump, rather than a tree (the relic is quite deceased, a victim, not of the shoe ritual, but of its swampy situation), the shoe tree is covered with discarded footwear: tennis shoes, wedding shoes and baby shoes; loafers, pumps and sandals. Shoes of all makes and sizes, styles and colors. The meaning of the shoe tree is obscure and almost certainly unrecorded, but I think it is a kind of primitive greeting: a welcome to all weary "soles" and a promise of a journey's end.

74   TLC10262 Copyright © Teaching & Learning Company, Carthage, IL 62321-0010

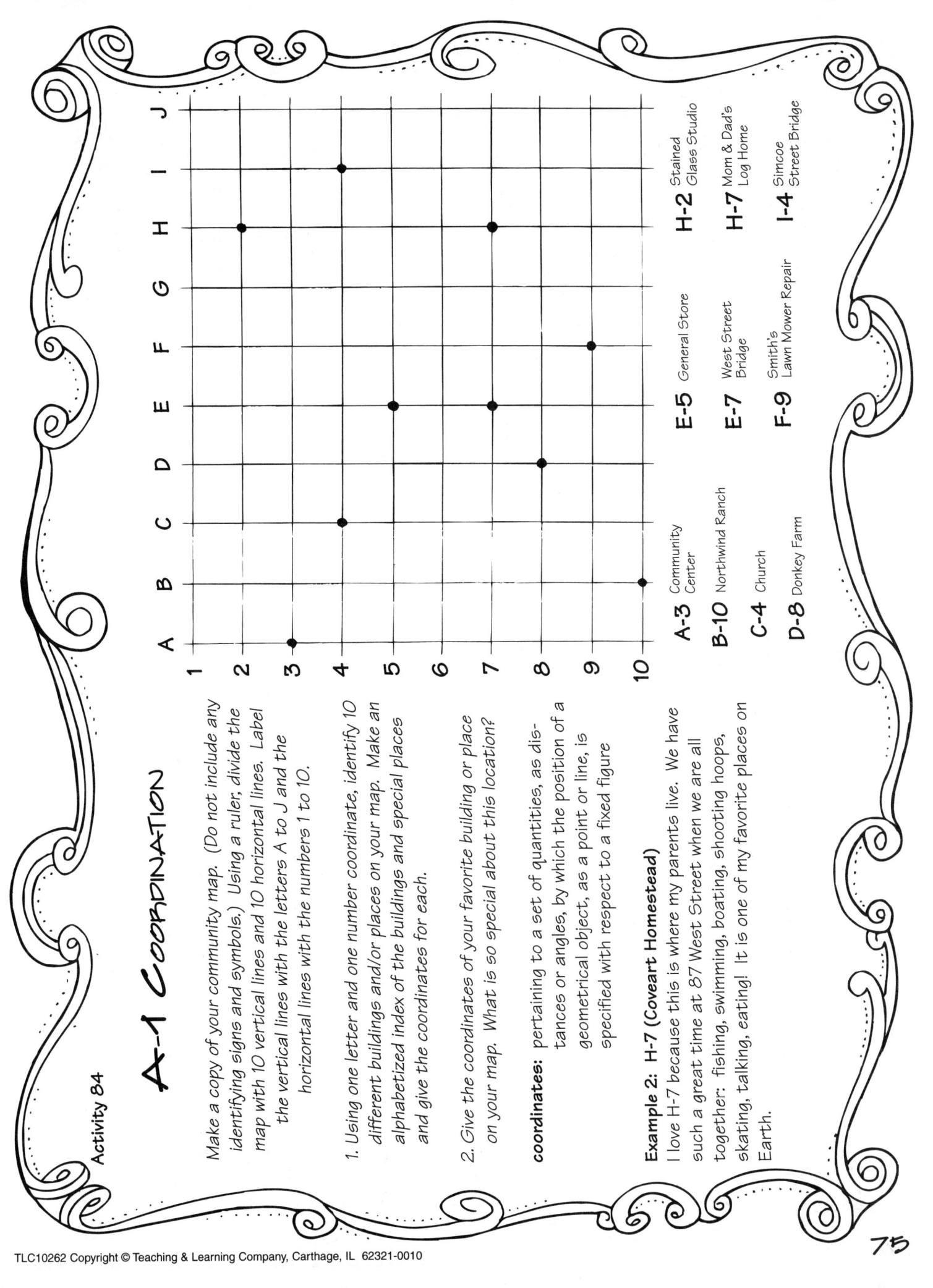

Activity 85

No Place Like Home

Describe your home. What is your favorite feature? What would you like to change? How long have you lived at your current address? What do you like most about living at this address? What do you like least?

Draw a picture of your home (or a room or special place in your home) and label the important or interesting parts.

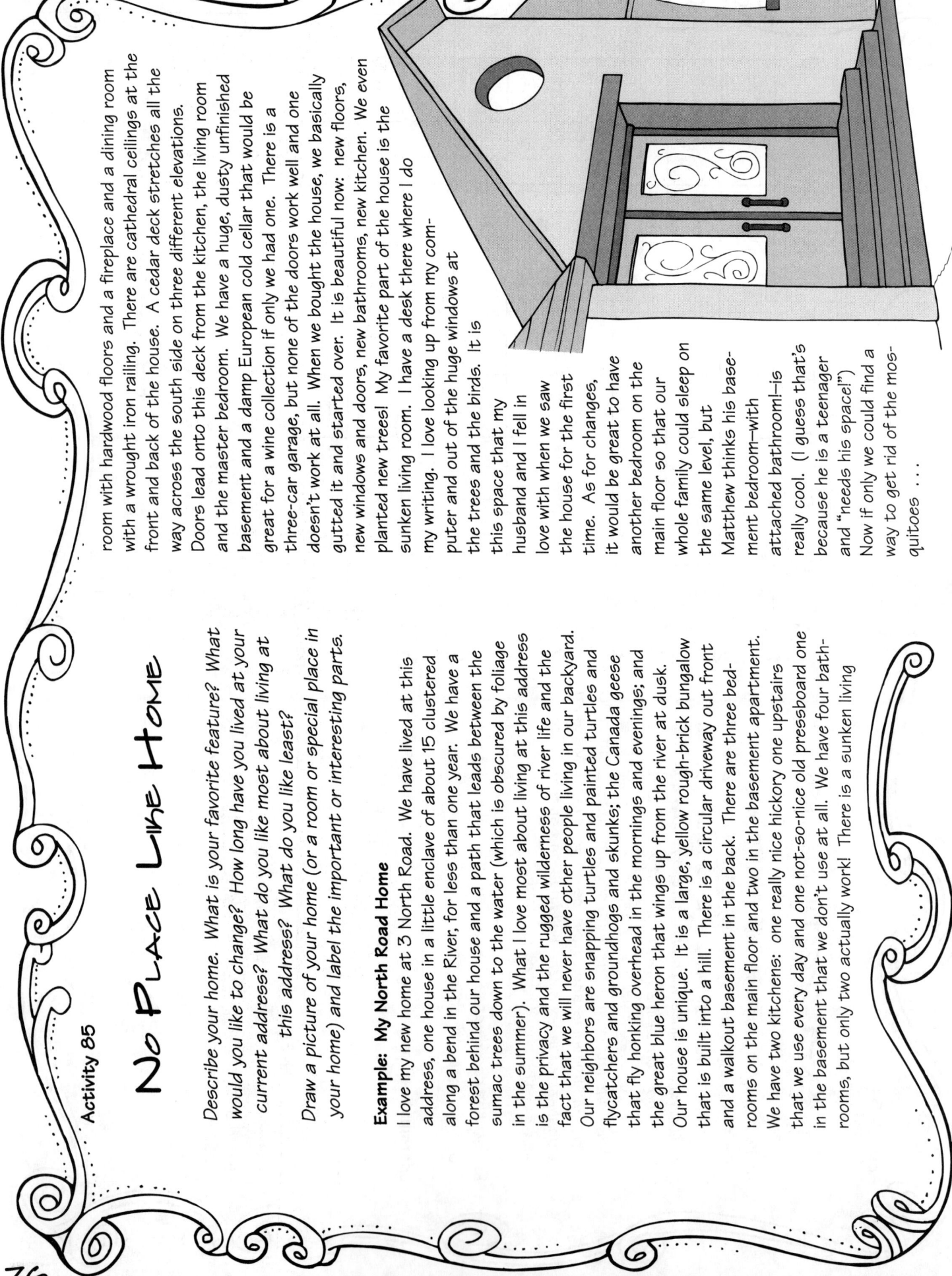

Example: My North Road Home

I love my new home at 3 North Road. We have lived at this address, one house in a little enclave of about 15 clustered along a bend in the River, for less than one year. We have a forest behind our house and a path that leads between the sumac trees down to the water (which is obscured by foliage in the summer). What I love most about living at this address is the privacy and the rugged wilderness of river life and the fact that we will never have other people living in our backyard. Our neighbors are snapping turtles and painted turtles and flycatchers and groundhogs and skunks; the Canada geese that fly honking overhead in the mornings and evenings; and the great blue heron that wings up from the river at dusk. Our house is unique. It is a large, yellow rough-brick bungalow that is built into a hill. There are three bedrooms on the main floor and two in the basement apartment. We have two kitchens: one really nice hickory one upstairs that we use every day and one not-so-nice old pressboard one in the basement that we don't use at all. We have four bathrooms, but only two actually work! There is a sunken living room with hardwood floors and a fireplace and a dining room with a wrought iron railing. There are cathedral ceilings at the front and back of the house. A cedar deck stretches all the way across the south side on three different elevations. Doors lead onto this deck from the kitchen, the living room and the master bedroom. We have a huge, dusty unfinished basement and a damp European cold cellar that would be great for a wine collection if only we had one. There is a three-car garage, but none of the doors work well and one doesn't work at all. When we bought the house, we basically gutted it and started over. It is beautiful now: new floors, new windows and doors, new bathrooms, new kitchen. We even planted new trees! My favorite part of the house is the sunken living room. I have a desk there where I do my writing. I love looking up from my computer and out of the huge windows at the trees and the birds. It is this space that my husband and I fell in love with when we saw the house for the first time. As for changes, it would be great to have another bedroom on the main floor so that our whole family could sleep on the same level, but Matthew thinks his basement bedroom—with attached bathroom!—is really cool. (I guess that's because he is a teenager and "needs his space!") Now if only we could find a way to get rid of the mosquitoes . . .

Activity 85

No Place Like Home
Continued

The Global Village

In this section, students develop an understanding of their place in the community and in the world. They look at life in urban and rural settings, discover cardinal directions and examine their dependence on the natural environment. They discuss the ways in which their community and country contribute to the global village and compare and contrast their lives to the lives of children in other parts of the world. Specifically, they . . .

- develop an understanding of the geographic location and the relevance of their home in a global context (Activities 86-87)
- develop a basic understanding of the cardinal directions (Activity 88)
- discriminate between urban and rural areas (Activity 89)
- develop an understanding of why people live where they do (Activity 90)
- examine interaction between communities (Activity 91)
- describe human dependence on the environment and ways in which people use the natural environment (Activity 92)
- discuss climate variation and how this affects lifestyle and the nature of basic human needs (Activity 93)
- describe resource depletion, pollution, extinction and the need for environmental awareness and protection at the global and individual levels (Activity 94)
- examine labels to discover the types of goods produced by other countries (Activity 95)
- discuss ways in which the sharing of goods and cross-cultural penetration influences their life-style (Activity 96)
- examine similarities and differences between their country and other countries (Activity 97)
- discuss their community's contribution to the gross national product and make a list of community exports using words and symbols (Activity 98)
- look at tourism and the reasons why people travel to other places (Activity 99)
- discuss their country's contributions to the global community (Activity 100)
- list the contents of a culturally/nationally significant time capsule (Activity 101)

Activity 86

A Small Part of the Big Picture

On a map of the world, color your continent.
On a map of your continent, color your country.
On a map of your country, color your state (or province).
On a map of your state (or province) put a colored dot to mark your city/town/village.
On a map of your city/town/village, color your street.
On your street, find the spot where your home should appear and mark it with a colored dot.

Arrange your maps so that they overlap one another in descending order (from larger to smaller, or "macro" to "micro"). Find a photograph of your home (or draw a picture of it) and put this at the bottom of your map file. The file should look like a series of photographs taken from space with a camera that zoomed in closer and closer with each frame, finally bringing the picture of your home into view.

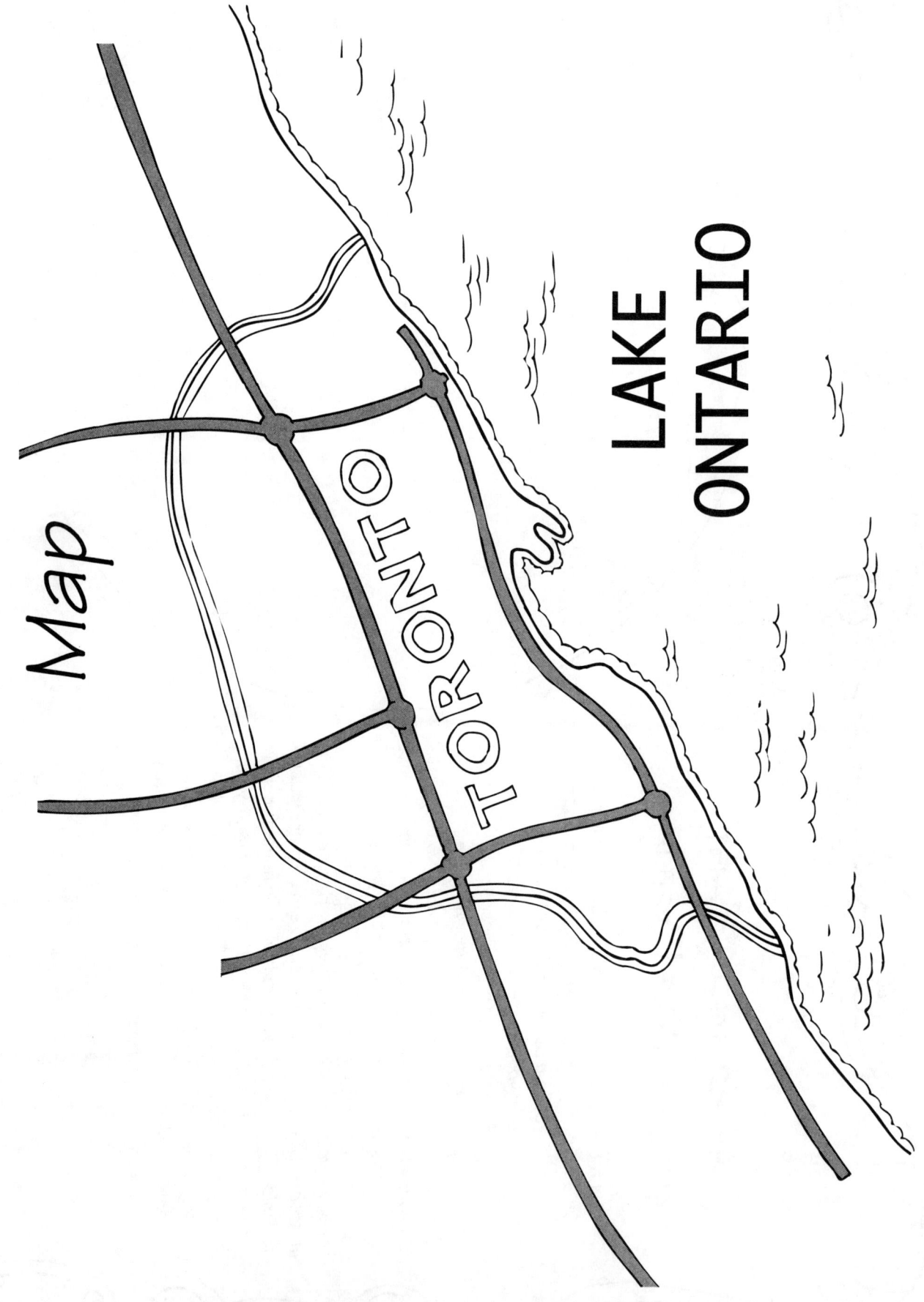

Activity 86

A Small Part of the Big Picture Map

West Street

West Street

River

my parents' property

Simcoe Street

North Road

N
W E
S

Activity 86

A Small Part of the Big Picture Map

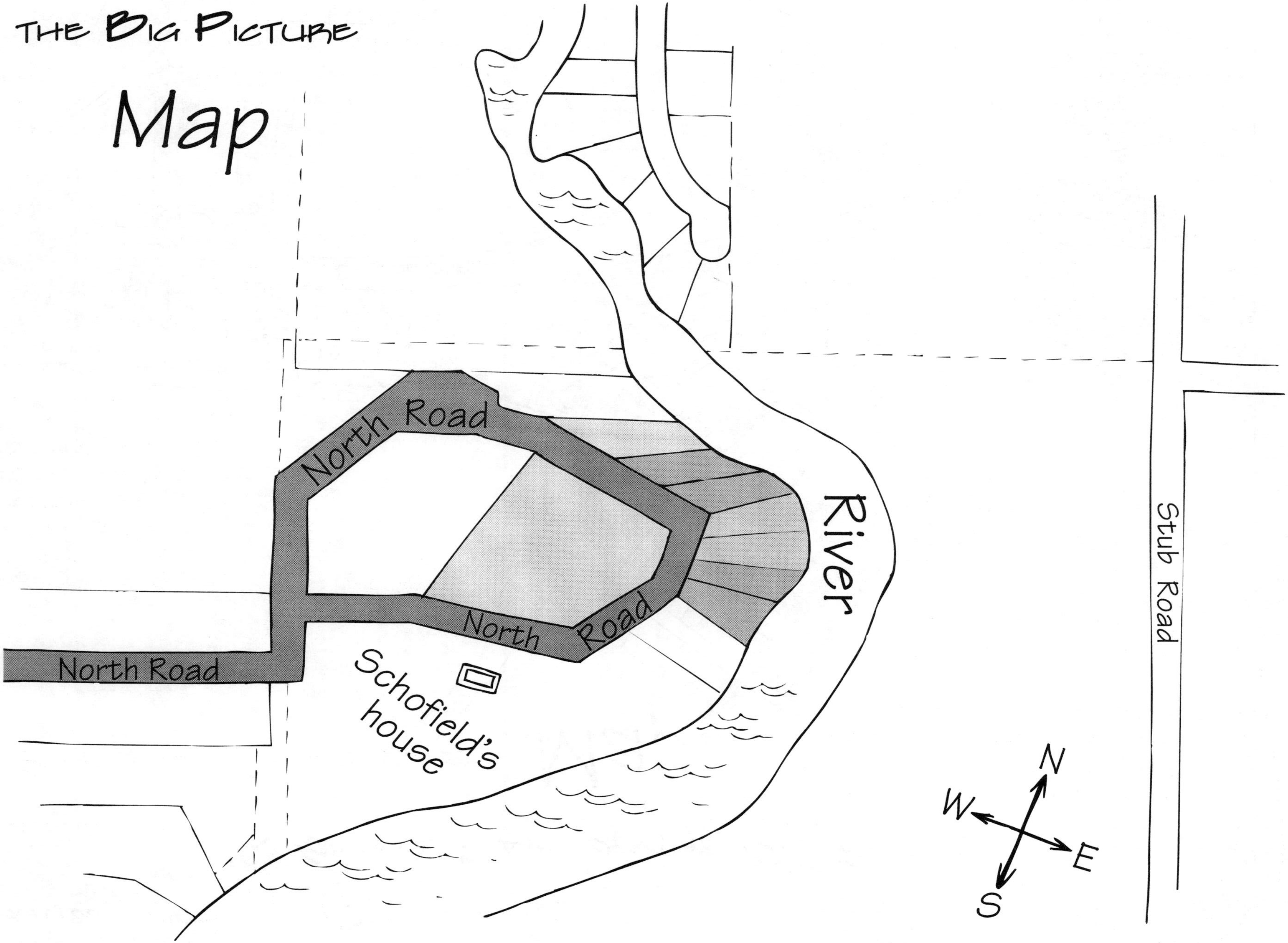

Stub Road

River

North Road

Schofield's house

N E S W

TLC10262 Copyright © Teaching & Learning Company, Carthage, IL 62321-0010

Activity 87

Popular Percentages

Every human being is a single "fish" that swims in the global ocean. Fill in the blanks below to understand how you are positioned in the context of the worldwide picture.

Geographic Location   **Est. Population**

Me (name): _____

My home (number): _____

My street: _____

My city/town/village: _____

My state/province: _____

My country: _____

My continent: _____

My planet: _____

What percentage of your street/town/state/country/continent/planet population does your household account for? To figure out these percentages, take the population of your household, divide by the population of your street/town/state/country/continent/planet and multiply this figure by 100. (You can use a calculator!)

Figure out some other percentages.

- You as a percentage of your household population, your street population, your city population, your state population, your national population, your continental population, the world population
- Your street's population as a percentage of the city population, the state population, the national population, the continental population, the world population
- Your city's population as a percentage of the state population, the continental population, the world population
- Your state's population as a percentage of the national population, the continental population, the world population
- Your country's population as a percentage of the continental population, the world population
- Your city's population as a percentage of the world population

Activity 87

Popular Percentages
CONTINUED

Example:

Geographic Location	Estimated Population*
Me: Tracey Schofield	1
My home: #3	5
My street: North Road	50
My city/town/village: My Town	500
My state/province: Ontario	11,513,808
My country: Canada	30,491,294
My continent: North America	308,966,949
My planet: Earth	7,000,000,000

*As of June 14, 2000

My Household
My household accounts for 10% of the population of my street (5 divided by 50 multiplied by 100 = 10%); 1% of the village population (5/500 × 100); 0.0000434% of my province's population (5/11,513,808 × 100) and 0.00001% of Canada's population (5/30,491,294 × 100).

My Village
My village accounts for 0.0000434% of my province's population and 0.0000163% of my country's population (5/30,491,294 × 100).

Activity 88

Never Eat Shredded Wheat (N, S, E, W)

Example: N, S, E, W of 3 Bank Road

Using the cardinal directions on your maps from Activity 86 (look for the small compass printed on each map), name a person, place or thing that can be found due north, east, south and west of your continent, country, state (province), city/town/village, street and home.

NORTH
Bob and Mary Jones
daughters Jenny, Janice and Jeanne
and dogs Muffin and Biscuit

EAST
a new golf course and waterfront housing development

SCHOFIELD HOME
3 North Road

WEST
My parents' property: 87 West St.

SOUTH
the river and "Old Smokey" (a great toboggan hill!)

Activity 89

The City Kid and the Country Kid

1. Divide your page into two columns, one labeled **Urban** and one labeled **Rural**. Down the left-hand margin, write the words: **physical features, land use, space, population/density, buildings, services, jobs and recreation**. Write your observations about each subject under the two headings. If you can think of any additional subjects for comparison, add them at the bottom of the row.

2. If you are an urbanite, what do you love about living in town? What appeals to you about life in the country? If you are a ruralist, what do you like most about living in the country? What might attract you to life in the big city? (If you are feeling adventurous, write your answers in the form of a story like "The City Mouse and the Country Mouse." Many versions of this story have already been published. Use your personal feelings, experience and style to rewrite an old tale with a new twist.)

Example: The Country Woman and Her City Brother

Once upon a time there was a woman who lived in the country. She loved rural life. She loved . . . .
The woman's brother lived in the city. He loved . . . .
One day, the woman's brother invited her to go and stay with him in the city. There was a big festival going on and he thought she might like to stay for a few days and take in some of the cultural activities. The woman was reluctant to leave her country home, but she did not want to hurt her brother's feelings, so she packed a bag, hopped on the bus and traveled into the city. It was . . .
The woman longed for her country home and the . . . that she loved so well. After one day, she told her brother she was feeling unwell and would have to leave. "Shall I drive you?" asked her brother. "That would be wonderful," the woman replied. "And we can continue our visit at my house. I will feel much improved as soon as the smog is cleared from my lungs." The brother agreed and the two set off. The brother looked longingly at the city he loved disappearing in his rearview mirror, but he didn't want to hurt his sister's feelings, so he pretended to be pleased. The very first night . . . .
After one day, the brother couldn't stand it anymore. He had to get back to the city. He told his sister that his partner had called on the cellular phone and notified him of an important meeting the next day. Sadly, he would have to go. His sister mouthed "good-bye" as his dusty BMW bumped its way over the potholes in her gravel driveway, windshield wipers waving madly back and forth in a desperate attempt to dislodge the bird droppings that were spattered across the glass. The woman and her brother kept in touch; but one ever proposed another visit. They preferred their long-distance relationship and let their voices do the travelling from that day forward, speeding back and forth between city and country through the telephone wires.

Author's Note: If I were writing a complete story, I would add detail after each ellipses.

Activity 90

Location, Location, Location!

It is a real estate catch phrase: location, location, location. But why do people live where they do?

1. How did your family come to live at its current address?
2. What factors might make people move from one place to another? What influences might encourage them to stay put? (Think of family ties, friendships and other personal relationships; jobs; stores and services; schools . . . .)

Example 1: From 'Burb to Village

My family disliked life in the suburbs intensely. We all wanted to live in the country, but our desire to move was tempered by some important considerations. We had to locate relatively close to Jonathan's place of work. We had a price limit. We did not want to be on or near a major roadway. We wanted acreage. We did not want to move any further away from my mom and dad. We wanted the benefits of small-town life but didn't want to be too far from amenities like grocery stores and pet shops. We needed to remain in our school zone. If any one of these criteria could not be satisfied, we could not have moved. Fortunately, 3 North Road, had check marks down the list, and . . . here we are!

Example 2: A Special Child

Our daughter, Stephanie, has special needs and where we live has a lot to do with how we can best meet these needs. Stephanie must be relatively close to the hospitals and medical specialists that she visits regularly. Schooling is another important consideration. The special educational program and environment in which she is currently doing so well is not available in every community or with every school board. We cannot have a house that is on a major roadway or one that allows easy access to water or other hazard. And most importantly, Stephanie needs to be near her extended family—her Nana and Papa—who offer her continuous support, encouragement, understanding and unconditional love.

Activity 91

Back and Forth

Although we live in one community, we rarely spend our entire lives within its confines. Traveling between communities is frequent, natural and even necessary.

1. Why might someone who lives in the country visit the city? Why might a city dweller travel to the country? (You're on your own for this activity!)

2. When was the last time you traveled to a different community? What was the purpose of your visit? What did you do while you were there?

Example: 2. Into TO
I travelled from my rural home to the city of Toronto just a few days ago. Unfortunately, I made the journey to attend a funeral. While I was in the city, I visited my aunt, who lives around the corner from the church. She took care of my daughter while my mom, my husband and I attended the service.

Activity 92

En-Dependent

If our planet where inhospitable, we could not inhabit it. We are dependent on the environment—the water, the soil and the air around us—to support life and to provide the essential ingredients for human existence.

1. List at least 10 ways that people are dependent on the environment. (Take it away!)

2. How do you and your family members use the natural environment?

Example: 2. Gone Fishin'
My two boys love fishing the river that runs along our property. Although they consider themselves anglers (catch and release types) rather than fishermen, they get immense recreational pleasure from this activity. (And, if we are ever desperately hungry, I am sure we could persuade them to keep, clean and cook what they catch!)

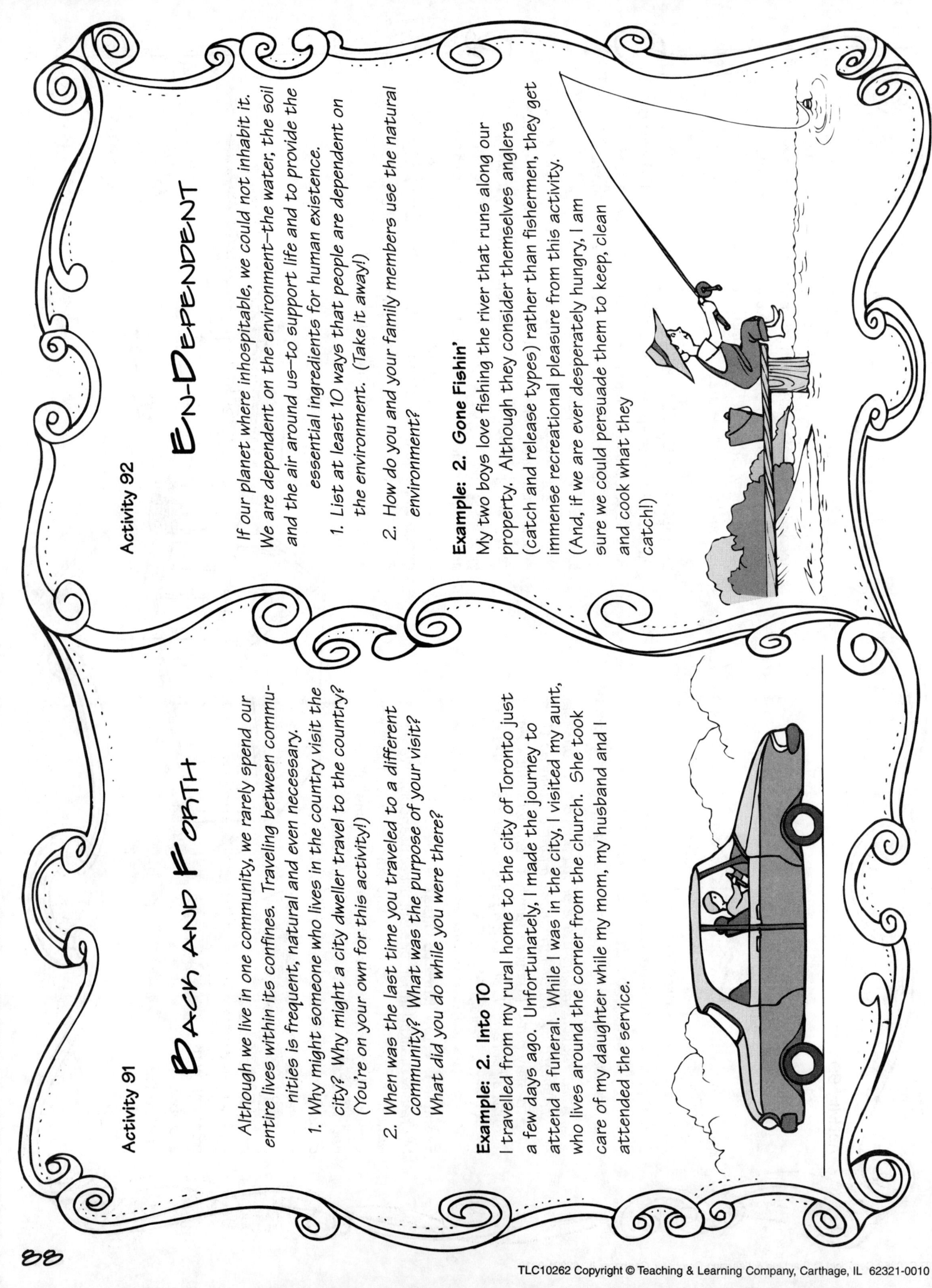

Activity 93

Climate Controlled

What we eat, what we wear, what we do and how we live are to a great extent determined by the climate in which we live. How does the climate exert influence over your life? Compare and contrast life in two different climatic zones. Choose from:

- Tropical climate (hot with rain all year): i.e. Singapore, Singapore
- Savanna climate (hot with dry season): i.e. Minna, Africa
- Steppe climate (warm and dry): i.e. Medicine Hat (Alberta), Canada
- Desert climate (hot and very dry): i.e. Bahrain, Bahrain
- Mild climate (warm and wet): i.e. Buenos Aires, Argentina
- Continental climate (wet with cold winter): i.e. Montreal (Quebec), Canada
- Subarctic climate (very cold winter): i.e. Irkutsk, Siberia
- Polar climate (very cold and dry): i.e. Eismitte, Greenland
- Mountainous climate (altitude affects climate): i.e. Addis Ababa, Ethiopia

Divide your page into two columns, headed with the two climates you are going to compare. Down the left-hand margin of the page, write the following considerations: housing, food, clothing, types of work, transportation and recreation. Based on your general knowledge, write several observations in each row under each column head. Can you think of any other considerations that you might be able to compare? If so, add them to your list.

Example:

	Tropical Climate	**Continental Climate**
Housing	no external heat source required	external heat source required for winter months
Food	available fresh year round	limited growing season and availability
Clothing	same all year	wardrobe changes according to season

Activity 94

Planet Protectors

Human beings take much from the Earth and give little back. We trade pollution for natural resources, habitation for wilderness, extinction for ecological diversity.

1. Write about one natural resource that is "running out." Why is it important that we take care of the environment? What might happen if we don't?

2. Look in a newspaper (or use your existing knowledge) to find out what your community, state or country is doing to help protect, preserve and improve the environment. Describe one initiative.

3. What can *you* do to help protect the environment and keep our planet healthy?

Example 2: Protecting the Nonquon Watershed
In my community, the amount of sewage that is dumped into the local holding ponds has been strictly limited to an amount that the natural Nonquon River system (which receives sewage water from the holding ponds for purification) can accommodate. This prevents the pollution of our waterway, protects wildlife and keeps the river—and the people who live along its banks—healthy.

Example 3: Swatting Flies
Sometimes the world's problems seem overwhelming. But each one of us can make a difference by contributing what we can to the larger solution. As an example, China was once overrun with houseflies. Rather than introduce a pest to deal with the flies or use a dangerous pesticide to kill them, the Chinese government issued each citizen a fly swatter and instructions to squash flies on sight. By empowering every man, woman and child to assume responsibility for the flies in his or her own household, the government was able to bring an end to the country's fly epidemic without harming the environment.

What if every man, woman and child was to pick up one piece of litter a day—or better yet, could refrain from throwing garbage on the ground in the first place?

Activity 95

Who Does What Where?

Look at the labels of at least 20 items in your kitchen, living room, closet or toy box. Where were these items produced or manufactured? Make a list of these items and their country of origin. Tally the number of items from each geographic location and graph your results with **Number of Items** on the vertical plane and **Place of Origin** on the horizontal plane.

Example: 10-Item Product/Origin List

Product	Origin
1. Danone Crystal Springs (water)	Piedmont, Quebec, Canada
2. Fanco Note Book	Montreal, Quebec, Canada
3. Cedco Calendar	San Rafael, California, USA
4. Hagen Aquarium Pebbles	Montreal, Quebec, Canada
5. Johnson's No More Tangles	Montreal, Quebec, Canada
6. Wardley Betta Food	Secaucus, New Jersey, USA
7. Gage Global Atlas	Toronto, Ontario, Canada
8. Original Clorets Gum	Scarborough, Ontario, Canada
9. Laura Secord Chocolates	North York, Ontario, Canada
10. Decorative light switch plate	Milton, Ontario, Canada

Tallies
- By city: Piedmont (1), Montreal (3), San Rafael (1), Secaucus (1), Toronto (1), Scarborough (1), North York (1), Milton (1)
- By state/province: Quebec (4), California (1), New Jersey (1), Ontario (4)
- By country: Canada (8), United States (2)

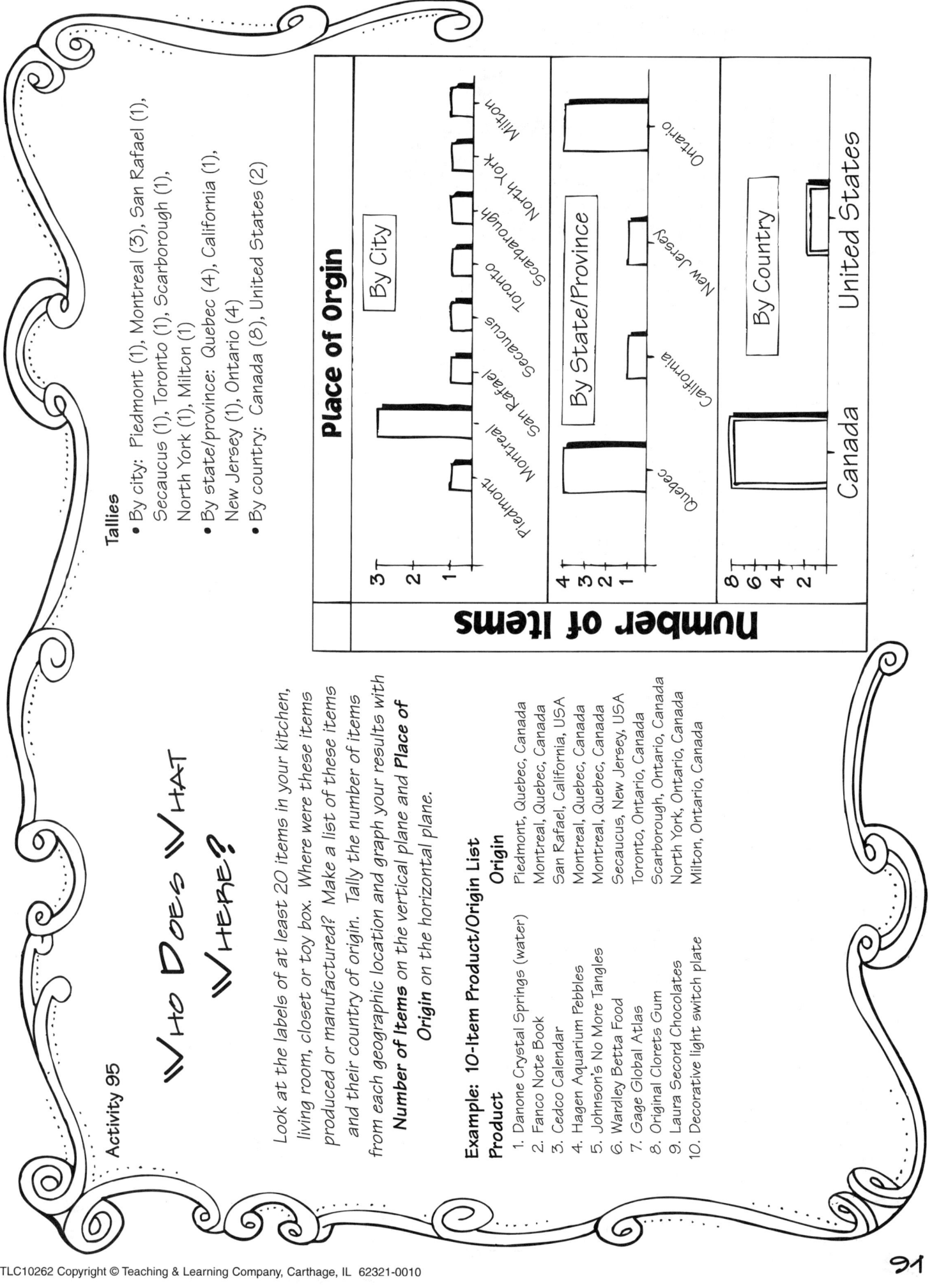

Activity 96

Trade-Offs

1. Think of one item of "foreign" merchandise (something that is made in another community, state/province or country and sold in yours) that has influenced or affected your life-style.

2. What is one item produced in your community, state/province or country and traded or sold to another that has altered or changed the way these consumers live? (You can consider past or present times in your answer.)

Example 1: Clorets from Scarborough

Evergreen Gum—with pine pellets—has changed my life. I used to worry a lot about my breath. Halitosis (a malodorous condition of the breath) runs in my family, and I was very self-conscious about the problem. Then I discovered Evergreen Gum, which "helps to fight mouth odor and gives you clean, fresh breath!" Manufactured in Needles, Ontario, by the Bough and Branch Company, Evergreen is one product that my mouth and I are glad we can buy.

Example 2: Indigenous Indians and Gunpowder

Thinking historically, the introduction of gunpowder to native North American Indians by white explorers and early settlers changed the traditional way of life of these indigenous people. Guns replaced the tribal bow and arrow as the hunting weapon of choice, altering forever the Indians' harmonious and balanced relationship with the natural environment.

Activity 97

One Big, Happy Family

Drawing on your knowledge of the world, think about the children of another country with which you are at least a little familiar.

1. How are you the same as these kids? How are you different? (I'm not going to help you here.)

2. What similarities are shared by all of humankind? Try writing your answer in poetic form: haiku, free verse, rhyming, list, concrete, acronym, etc.

Example:

The Human Family
(a Five Ws—or who, what, where, when and why—Poem)

People
Have lived and died
On this same Earth, beneath this same sun
Since time began
Because we all belong to the same, human family

Activity 98

Prodigious Producers

What "goods" does your family, community, state (province) or country produce? Make a picture list of at least 10 of these wares or articles. Label each drawing.

goods: merchandise; wares or articles bought and sold; commodities of trade

Example: Among other things, my rural community produces:

- beef
- milk
- corn
- soybeans
- apples
- wine
- handcrafted pine furniture
- pottery
- stained glass
- gourd birdhouses

Activity 99

Seeing the World

Around the world, tourism—traveling for recreation—is big business.

1. Why do you think people travel to other places?

2. If you could travel to five destinations, anywhere in the world, where would you go and why?

3. Survey the people in your household regarding their top five travel destinations. Tally the totals and plot them on a graph (with **Number of Wishful Visitors** on the vertical axis and **Dream Destinations** on the horizontal axis).

4. Optional Class Activity: Survey the kids in your class to find out their ultimate travel destinations. Tally the totals. Plot these on a graph with **Number of Kids** on the vertical axis and **Ultimate Travel Destination** on the horizontal axis. Which is the most popular travel destination? Compare your results to those in another class.

Example: 2. Tracey's Travels

I would like to visit: Scotland (to explore my celtic roots and cultural heritage–the Gordon clan fought at Culloden), England (to tour castles and historical villages), Rome (to see the Colosseum and other architectural artifacts of ancient civilization), Africa (to go on safari and get close to the wild animals I have grown up learning and yearning about) and Fiji (because I want to see white sand, crystal blue water and tropical fish that are not swimming in an aquarium or across my television screen).

Example: 3. Family Favorites

Tracey: Scotland, England, Rome, Africa and Fiji

Jonathan: England, Monaco, Australia, France and Africa

Matthew: USA (Florida), Tijuana, Africa, England and France

Patrick: USA (Florida), England, Australia, Africa and Canada (Rocky Mountains)

Stephanie: USA (Florida), Africa, Australia, Fiji, Canada (Rocky Mountains)

Tallies

- Africa (5), England (4), USA (3), Australia (3), Fiji (2), France (2), Canada (2), Scotland (1), Rome (1), Monaco (1), Tijuana (1)

Activity 100

Conscientious Contributions

Use your existing knowledge or look in a newspaper to find out how your community, state/province or country contributes to the global community.

What does your community, state/province or country do to help other countries?

Activity 101

Time in a Bottle

Imagine that you are putting together a time capsule that will be launched into space.

1. What 10 things would you like the extraterrestrial who finds your capsule to know about you, your community, your country and your planet? (Consider the past, present and future in your answer.)

2. What 20 items would you include in the time capsule that would help to explain life, as you know it, to intergalactic explorers?

Answer Key

Activity 1
Social Studies Word Search
Page 5

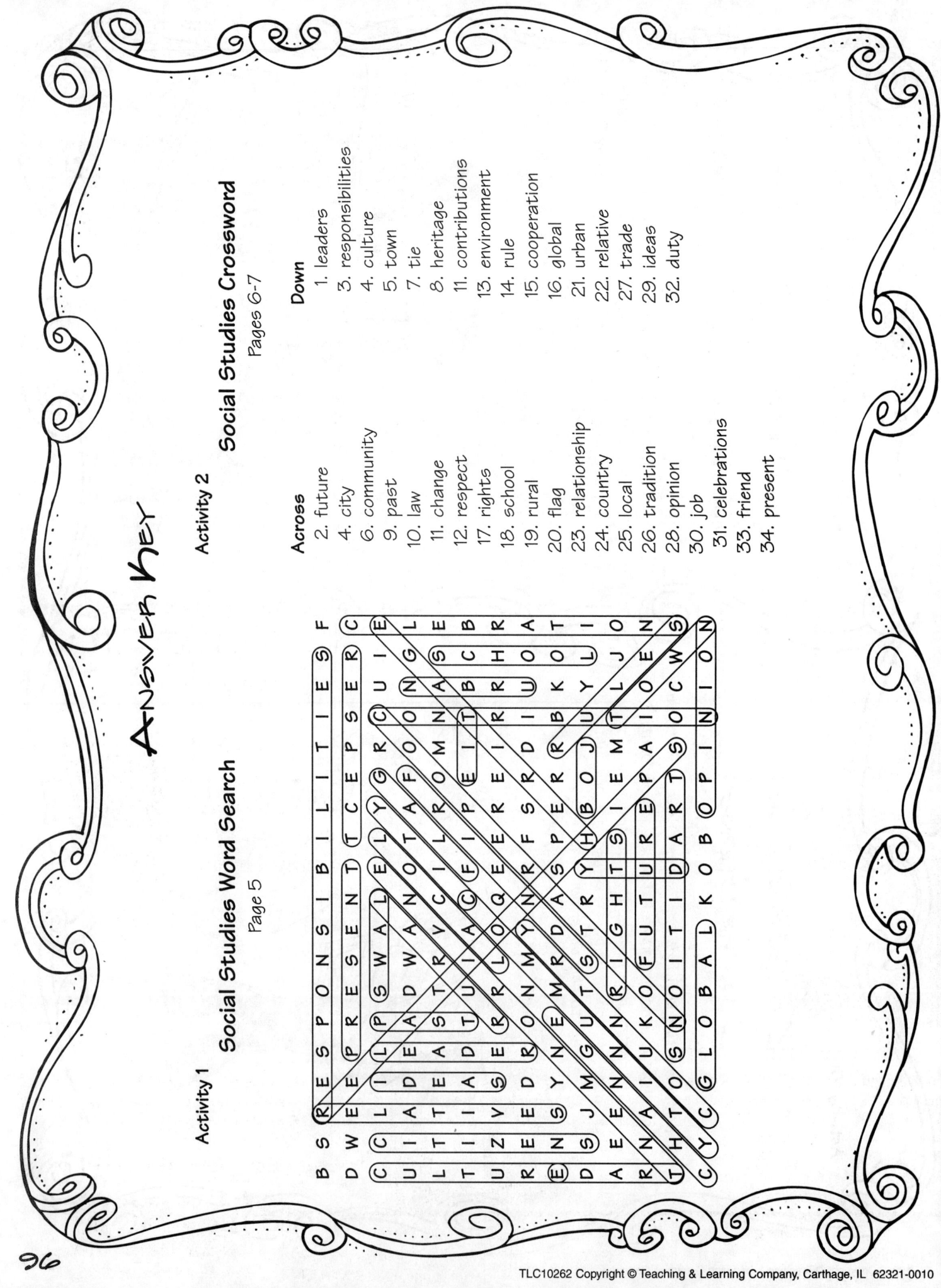

Activity 2
Social Studies Crossword
Pages 6-7

Across
2. future
4. city
6. community
9. past
10. law
11. change
12. respect
17. rights
18. school
19. rural
20. flag
23. relationship
24. country
25. local
26. tradition
28. opinion
30. job
31. celebrations
33. friend
34. present

Down
1. leaders
3. responsibilities
4. culture
5. town
7. tie
8. heritage
11. contributions
13. environment
14. rule
15. cooperation
16. global
21. urban
22. relative
27. trade
29. ideas
32. duty